Dorothy Parker

ALSO BY BARRY DAY

My Life with Noël Coward *(with Graham Payn)*
This Wooden 'O': Shakespeare's Globe Reborn
Noël Coward: The Complete Lyrics *(editor and annotator)*
Noël Coward: A Life in Quotes *(editor)*
Noël Coward: Collected Sketches and Parodies *(editor)*
The Theatrical Companion to Coward, Updated Edition
    (coedited with Sheridan Morley)
The Unknown Noël: New Writing from the Coward Archive
    (editor)
Oscar Wilde: A Life in Quotes *(editor)*
P. G. Wodehouse: In His Own Words *(coedited with Tony Ring)*
Sherlock Holmes: In His Own Words and the Words of Those
    Who Knew Him *(editor)*
Sherlock Holmes and the Shakespeare Globe Murders
Sherlock Holmes and the Alice in Wonderland Murders
Sherlock Holmes and the Copycat Murders
Sherlock Holmes and the Apocalypse Murders
Sherlock Holmes and the Seven Deadly Sins Murders
Murder, My Dear Watson *(contributor)*

PLAYS:

Aspects of Oscar
Noël&Alfred&Lynn
"As Dorothy Parker Once Said . . ."
The Ten Year Lunch: The Algonquin Round Table
Waltz of My Heart: The Life and Music of Ivor Novello
Noël Coward's After the Ball *(concert adaptation)*
Noël Coward's Pacific 1860 *(concert adaptation)*
Oh, Boy! *(concert adaptation)*
King's Rhapsody *(concert adaptation)*

Dorothy Parker

In Her Own Words

Edited by Barry Day

TAYLOR TRADE PUBLISHING
Lanham • New York • Dallas • Boulder • Toronto • Oxford

Published by Taylor Trade Publishing
An imprint of The Rowman & Littlefield Publishing Group, Inc.
4501 Forbes Boulevard, Suite 200
Lanham, Maryland 20706

Distributed by National Book Network

Library of Congress Cataloging-in-Publication Data

Parker, Dorothy, 1893-1967
    Dorothy Parker, in her own words / edited by Barry Day.— 1st Taylor
Trade Publishing ed.
      p. cm.
    ISBN 1-58979-071-5 (hardcover : alk. paper)
    1. Parker, Dorothy, 1893–1967. 2. Authors, American—20th century—
Biography. I. Day, Barry. II. Title.
PS3531.A5855Z47 2004
818'.5209—dc22   2003023793

For Lynne . . .
(My Own FLB)

Contents

Acknowledgments

I would like to thank Viking Penguin (a division of Penguin Group USA Inc.) and the National Association for the Advancement of Colored People for authorizing this use of Dorothy Parker's works. Specifically . . .

From THE PORTABLE DOROTHY PARKER by Dorothy Parker, edited by Brendan Gill, copyright 1928, renewed © 1956 by Dorothy Parker. Used by permission of Viking Penguin, a division of Penguin Group USA Inc.

From DOROTHY PARKER COMPLETE STORIES by Dorothy Parker, copyright 1924-29, 1931-34, 1937-39, 1941, 1943, 1955, 1958, 1995 by The National Association for the Advancement of Colored People. Used by permission of Penguin, a division of Penguin Group USA Inc.

From DOROTHY PARKER: COMPLETE POEMS by Dorothy Parker, copyright © 1999 by The National Association for the Advancement of Colored People. Used by permission of Penguin, a division of Penguin Group USA Inc.

Dorothy Parker's letter to Alexander Woollcott is used by permission of the Houghton Library, Harvard University.

The lyrics of the song "I Wished On the Moon" are reproduced by permission of the Hal Leonard Corporation.

The painting *A Vicious Circle* by Natalie Ascensios is reproduced by permission of the Algonquin Hotel.

I would also like to thank the following individuals and organizations for their help with this project: Florence Eichin (Penguin Group USA); Lynn Slawson (Gordon Feinblatt, Rothman, Hoffberger & Hollander, LLC); the New York Public Library; Leslie Morris (Houghton Library); Dave Johnstone & Jim Heineman of The Algonquin Hotel, New York; Ray Wemmlinger (Hampden-Booth Library); The Players, New York.

I have made every effort to locate copyright owners and any I may have been unable to find will be given due recognition in future editions of this book.

Introduction

My life is like a picture gallery,
With narrow aisles wherein the spectators may walk....
My life is like a picture gallery,
With a few pictures turned discreetly to the wall.

—"The Picture Gallery"

Rather than write my life story I would cut my throat
with a dull knife.

—Dorothy Parker to Quentin Reynold

LIKE MANY WRITERS whose specialty is the satirical observation of others, Dorothy Parker never wrote an autobiography. Perhaps the apparent incongruity of seeming to take themselves seriously after a lifetime of debunking has something to do with it.

At times she would say she was thinking about it. "I'd never be able to do it, but I wish to God I could; I'd like to write the damned thing, just so I could call it *Mongrel*." Then, late in life, she agreed to journalist Wyatt Cooper's suggestion that he would help her by having her talk into a tape recorder. "It would give me something to live for," she replied, with the caveat, "Let's make it gay; if it's not fun, there's no point in telling it."

Cooper was optimistic—until the tape started turning. Then the Dickensian anecdotes crowded in: "I apologize for introducing nobody but dreadful characters." And the irrelevance started pouring. The monologue was, as Wyatt put it, "replete with things that, in a more collected moment, she would never have said." He suppressed the tapes and gave up the task. In more ways than one, the moment for Dorothy Parker to tell her own story had passed.

In any case, she had already told it—carefully, covertly, and with sly, downcast eye—in and between the lines of her published writings. Somehow, there was a certain personal privacy within the rigorous discipline of a verse form—hadn't Shakespeare shown that with his sonnets? And the one-to-one asides with the readers of "Constant Reader" allowed you to throw a few biographical crumbs on the water and see if they were gobbled up before they sank. The printed page was her confessional.

In everything she wrote, she spoke with her own quiet wry voice, even when the things she said were patently outrageous. Always there was the invisible cloak of irony to protect her. "Can't you fellows take a joke? Where's your sense of humour?"

Humor, to her, was the sine qua non of a civilized society. "The possession of a sense of humour," she wrote in 1931, "entails the sense of selection, the civilized fear of going too far. . . . It keeps you, from your respect for the humor of others, from making a dull jackass of yourself. Humor, imagination and manners are pretty fairly interchangeably interwoven." And Dorothy Parker was never noticeably deficient in the first two—although the latter could have used a little attention from time to time.

Together they helped secure for her the reputation as being the greatest wit since Wilde. So much so that the lyric in a 1920s Broadway revue could include the lines

No matter who said it,
Dorothy Parker gets the credit.

Like Wilde, she may well have been at her best in conversation—
but there the resemblance ended. Wilde would deliver his bons
mots with mellifluous deliberation. Mrs. Parker would adopt a
demure deadpan expression, then proceed in her quiet, cultured
voice to mouth carefully articulated near-obscenities—usually in
the form of a riposte. Coming from a woman, the effect was even
more shocking.

People learned it was well to be wary of her. Tallulah
Bankhead, who liked her despite many a putdown, called her "the
mistress of the verbal hand grenade"; Robert Sherwood referred
to her as a "stiletto made of sugar"; Mrs. Patrick Campbell spoke
of "a pretty, pretty cobra" and Anita Loos of "a lone wolverine";
and Alexander Woollcott declared, "It is not so much the familiar phenomenon of a hand of steel in a velvet glove as a lacy
sleeve with a bottle of vitriol concealed in its folds."

Her sardonic romanticism, the side-of-the-mouth "Hey,
what can you expect?" cynicism, and her "urban voice" were certainly a typical product of the 1920s, but her work has never
really dated—despite her assertion that it would—because the
underlying *attitude* has proved to be a fundamental defense
against personal and social angst. Today—even more than then—
a primary concern is to be "cool," to have seen it all and risen
above it.

Thus, there are lines in Dorothy Parker that continue to
strike a chord for almost every beleaguered one of us. Next to
Wilde, she must be one of the most quoted (and misquoted) of
writers. What one misses, though, by picking up the individual
jewels is the unique context in which they are set. Read her work
in total, and a striking personal portrait emerges of a woman
perpetually drawn to but disillusioned by love; highly suspicious
of good news and the messengers who bring it; self-mocking,
self-loathing, and deliberately underachieving; lonely and constantly contemplating death and the means of achieving it, her

eye perpetually peeled for the dark cloud that invariably accompanies any silver lining.

Barely below the surface, flippancy is as naked and disturbing a portrait of another human being as one is likely to see. But for all her apparent manic-depressive moods, the silver lining persisted in reappearing. "I am," she wrote, "the greatest little hoper that ever lived."

"She was part of nothing and nobody except herself," said her friend Lillian Hellman at her funeral. "It was this independence of mind and spirit that was her true distinction."

If she had an unconscious role model, it might well have been Becky Sharp from her beloved *Vanity Fair*—the beautiful but inherently bad girl who continues to fascinate all who meet her. Time and again, one is left with the feeling that Dorothy Parker feels the need to check herself to make sure that her claws have not lost their edge. If anyone should start to pigeonhole her as simply a sweet little lady who writes little verses, she'll show *them*. . . .

There was little about her that was simple. Her verbal potential, in particular, was virtually limitless. "By God, I *read* . . . !" she would say about her school days, and one can sense the eclectic nature of her reading in the passage from "The Little Hours" in which the insomniac heroine decides that it might help her to sleep if she were to "repeat to myself, slowly and soothingly, a list of quotations beautiful from minds profound; if I can remember any of the damn things. . . .

"Oh, yes, I know one. This above all, to thine own self be true and it must follow, as the night the day, thou canst not then be false to any man. Now they're off. And once they get started, they ought to come like hot cakes. Let's see. They also serve who only stand and wait. If Winter comes, can Spring be far behind? Lilies that fester smell far worse than weeds. Silent upon a peak in Darien. Mrs. Porter and her daughter wash their feet in soda-water. And Agatha Arth is a hug-the-hearth, but my true love is false. Why did you die when lambs were cropping, you should

have died when apples were dropping. Shall be together, breathe
and ride, so one day more am I deified, who knows but the world
will end tonight. And he shall hear the stroke of eight and not
the stroke of nine. They are not long, the weeping and the laughter; love and desire and hate I think will have no portion in us
after we pass the gate. But none, I think, do there embrace. I
think that I shall never see a poem lovelier than a tree. I think I
will not hang myself today. Ay tank Ay go home now."

In that one passage, she embraces *Hamlet*, Walter Savage
Landor, Milton, Shelley, Shakespeare's sonnets, Keats, Eliot,
Dowson, Marvell, Alfred Joyce Kilmer (*who?*), and Chesterton.
Along the way she also manages to touch on all the main themes
of her work—before finally pulling the rug.

*D*orothy Parker: In Her Own Words draws from her own published writings, her letters, and the memories of others—
flawed or otherwise. It may not be her autobiography as she
would have selectively written it, but it is hers the way she spoke
it. And *Mongrel* would not have done her justice.

Barry Day
Connecticut 2004

"A Little Jewish Girl Trying to Be Cute"

*All those writers who talk about their childhood!
Gentle God, if I ever wrote about mine, you wouldn't
sit in the same room with me.*

—Dorothy Parker

*Boy, did I think I was smart! . . . I was just a little
Jewish girl trying to be cute.*

—Dorothy Parker

"IT WAS THE last time I was early for anything."
Dorothy Parker speaking about her premature arrival
into the world on August 22, 1893, two months before
she was expected. Born Dorothy Rothschild—the second daughter of a Jewish father and a Catholic mother—she was always
exercised by the racial mixture in her—to the point where she
threatened to call her autobiography (should she ever write one)

I

Dorothy Parker in 1921.

Mongrel. And just in case anyone was thinking—"My God, no, dear! We'd never even *heard* of *those* Rothschilds."

It was not a name she cared for. When asked why she married her first husband, Edwin Pond Parker II, she was, for once, in total earnest when she replied, "I married him to change my name." Even after she had divorced him, she insisted on retaining his name. Why was she called "Mrs." Parker? "Well, you see, there *was* a Mr. Parker."

Her Jewish ancestry was something she rarely referred to, and it was certainly never the subject of her own humor. Most of her friends respected the fact—a rare exception being George S. Kaufman on one occasion at the Algonquin Round Table. Pretending to be offended at some anti-Semitic remark, Kaufman— a successful Jewish writer with whom Parker was never particularly friendly—rose to his feet and claimed that he was leaving. "And I'll expect Mrs. Parker to accompany me. Halfway."

Another bone of personal contention was that the woman who was to become the quintessential New Yorker was actually born in *New Jersey*, of all places—West End, New Jersey, to be precise.

"You see, I have always lived in New York," she would write in 1921. "I was cheated out of the distinction of being a native New Yorker, because I had to go and get born while the family was spending the Summer in New Jersey, but, honestly, we came back into town right after Labor Day, so I nearly made the grade. When I was a little girl—which was along about the time that practically nobody was safe from Indians—I was insular beyond belief. At Summer resorts, I would ask my new playmates, 'What street do you live on?' I never said, 'What town do you live in?'"

The New York family home was a substantial house on West 72nd Street. "It's still standing, I believe," she said in an early 1960s interview, adding, "They sell trusses there now." She had always loved the urban landscape, although, "if I go above 72nd Street, I get a nosebleed!"

She said of her home town: "There comes to me the sharp picture of New York at its best, on a shiny, blue-and-white Autumn day with its buildings cut diagonally in half of light and shadow, with its straight, neat avenues colored with quick throngs, like confetti in the breeze. . . . I see New York at holiday time, always in the late afternoon, under a Maxfield Parrish sky, with the crowds even more quick and nervous but even more good-natured, the dark groups splashed with the white of Christmas packages, the lighted, holly-strung shops urging them in to buy more and more. I see it on a Spring morning, with the clothes of the women as soft and as hopeful as the pretty new leaves on a few, brave trees. I see it at night with the low skies red with the back-flung lights of Broadway, those lights of which Chesterton—or they told me it was Chesterton—said, 'What a marvelous sight for those who cannot read!' I see it in the rain, I smell the enchanting odor of wet asphalt, with the empty streets black and shining like wet olives. I see it—by this time, I become maudlin with nostalgia—even with its gray mounds of crusted snow, its little Appalachians of ice along the pavements. . . . I suppose that is the thing about New York. It is always a little more than you had hoped for."

The "family" consisted of her parents, two older brothers, and an older sister, Helen. "There were nine years between my sister and me . . . she was a real beauty; sweet, lovely, but silly." They were to remain close until Helen's death in 1944 at the age of fifty-seven.

It was a different story with her brothers.

"I remember my brother coming along the street once with a friend. The friend pointed at me. 'That your sister?' 'No,' my brother said. That helped. There was an enormous gap there, you see. You can't bridge that, ever." There is no evidence that in adult life she bothered to try.

In that very different late Victorian era—in which the New Jersey shore was considered a fashionable summer place for a middle-class family—one naturally had servants. The Rothschilds made a habit of employing exclusively Irish servants.

"My parents used to go down to Ellis Island and bring them, still bleeding, home to do the laundry. You know, that didn't encourage them to behave well. Honest, it didn't."

In July 1897, when Dorothy was nearly five, Eliza Rothschild "promptly went and died on me," and, as young children often do, Dorothy began to believe that somehow her mother's death was her fault. Within two years, Henry Rothschild had remarried. His second wife was a forty-something retired schoolteacher, Eleanor Lewis, a lady of somewhat rigid demeanor, by all accounts, who most definitely did not hit it off with the Rothschild children.

"She was hurt because the older ones called her 'Mrs. Rothschild.' What else? That was her name. I didn't call her anything. 'Hey, you' was about the best I could do.

"She was crazy with religion. I'd come in from school and she'd greet me with, 'Did you love Jesus today?' Now, how do you answer that?"

Her relationship with her father was ambivalent, especially after the hasty remarriage. She found the quality of his grief over her departed mother distinctly questionable.

"On Sundays he'd take us on an outing. Some outing. We'd go to the cemetery to visit my mother's grave. All of us, including the second wife. That was his idea of a treat. Whenever he'd hear a crunch of gravel that meant an audience approaching, out would come the biggest handkerchief you ever saw and, in a lachrymose voice that had remarkable carrying power, he'd start wailing, 'We're all here, Eliza! I'm here. Dottie's here. Mrs. Rothschild is here.'"

In 1903, the second Mrs. Rothschild dropped dead of a brain hemorrhage, and now the ten-year-old Dorothy had *two* "murders" on her conscience. It was small wonder that loving mothers did not feature in major roles in her subsequent fiction.

Her first school was a convent, the Blessed Sacrament Academy in New York City. "It was practically round the corner," and—the qualification that seemingly endeared it to Mr. Rothschild—"you didn't have to cross any avenues, whatever that means. Never mind you wouldn't learn anything.

"Convents do the same thing progressive schools do, only they don't know it. They don't teach you how to read, you have to figure that out for yourself. At my convent we did have a text-book, one that devoted a page and a half to Adelaide Ann Proctor, but we couldn't read Dickens; he was vulgar, you know. But I read him and Thackeray, and I'm the one woman you'll know who's read every word of Charles Reade, the author of *The Cloister and the Hearth*. But as for helping in the outside world, the convent taught me only that if you spit on a pencil eraser it will erase ink."

And as for her fellow pupils, "They weren't exactly your starched crinoline set, you know. Dowdiest little bunch you ever saw.

"I remember little else about it, except the smell of the oil-cloth, and the smell of the nuns' garb. All those writers who talk about their childhood! Gentle God, if I ever wrote about mine, you wouldn't sit in the same room with me."

And she never did. Nor did the episode end happily, for Mr. Rothschild was asked to remove his daughter forthwith from the consecrated ground.

"I was fired for a lot of things. . . . Well, how do you *expect* them to treat a kid who saw fit to refer to the Immaculate Conception as 'Spontaneous Combustion'? Boy, did I think I was smart! Still do."

She was sent to Miss Dana's Academy in Morristown, New Jersey—an accidentally symbolic return to roots? Her new school-mates were, she found, "congenitally equipped with a restfully unenquiring mind." The Dana Girl "had a general air, no matter how glorious the weather, of being dressed in expectation of heavy rains."

At Miss Dana's, she was at least allowed to read, and "by God, I read." It was here she discovered Horace, Virgil, Catullus, Aristotle, Socrates, Martial, Goethe, Montaigne, and a recently deceased kindred spirit, Oscar Wilde. She also read Verlaine and presumably Rimbaud—since she was later to remark that the homosexual French poet "was always chasing Rimbauds." And it was also in these years that at least the *name* of La Rochefoucauld made its indelible mark on the Parker mind.

In her story "The Little Hours" (1933), the insomniac heroine's mind wanders through a random list of options. Would it help her to sleep if she were to *read*? But no.

"All the best minds have been off reading for years. Look at the swing La Rochefoucauld took at it. He said that if nobody learned to read, very few people would be in love. There was a man for you, and that's what *he* thought of it. Good for you, La Rochefoucauld; nice going, boy. I wish *I'd* never learned to read."

But later the repetitive memory of her hero begins to pall.

"Let them keep their La Rochefoucauld, and see if I care. I'll stick to La Fontaine. Only I'd be better company if I could quit thinking that La Fontaine married Alfred Lunt."

She also began to write herself—a fact that caused her to examine her own handwriting and remark optimistically in a 1906 letter to her father, "They say when your writing goes uphill, you have a hopeful disposition. Guess I have." There is no record of his reply. Most people who knew her in later life would almost certainly have disputed her interpretation, though she herself would continue to insist, "I'm the greatest little hoper that ever lived."

Insofar as she was capable, she seems to have been happy during her time at Miss Dana's, for there was at least some stability to her existence that her home life failed to provide. Allowing for the tongue in the Parker cheek, one can interpret a remark like "I, too, can remember those roseate days of happy girlhood when we used to skulk off to attend dramas, thinking that we were seeing life. Ah, youth, youth" as being a reasonably positive verdict.

She does not appear to have made close friends. Possibly her tongue kept likely candidates at a distance. Even then, she was able to close off an unwanted conversation with a pithy line delivered with quiet finality.

"Are you my best friend?" a classmate in the convent asked her. To which Miss Rothschild is supposed to have replied, "A girl's best friend is her mutter." To which there is no answer for a less articulate child.

Throughout her subsequent life, Dorothy Parker was prone to turn her own version of it into an effective anecdote or—particularly—a telling line. As a result, we probably need to take the saga of the unfeeling father, the heartless stepmother, and the caricature nuns with a pinch of proverbial salt.

What is certain is that her formal education ended in the fall of 1908 at the age of fourteen. After that, she stayed at home—a situation that was by no means uncommon for young ladies of the period. Five years later, her father died, too.

"After my father died, there wasn't any money. I had to work, you see."

"Brevity Is the Soul of Lingerie"

Brevity Is the Soul of Lingerie

—*Vogue* caption

I hate the Office;
It cuts in on my social life.

—"Our Office—A Hate Song"

Three be the things I shall have till I die:
Laughter and hope and a sock in the eye.

—"Inventory"

I N 1914, Dorothy Parker began to make a little money playing a piano ("single notes") at a dance school and even
teaching dancing ("about which I knew nothing"). At least
the experience taught her all the current song hits, which would

come in handy in later years when she tried her hand at composing them. She also published—and was paid for—her first piece of that verse in the prestigious Condé Nast magazine *Vanity Fair*.

Her savior was Frank Crowninshield, who ran both *Vanity Fair* and its sister magazine, *Vogue*.

"Mr. Crowninshield, God rest his soul, paid twelve dollars for a small verse of mine and gave me a job [at *Vogue*] at ten dollars a week. Well, I thought I was Edith Sitwell."

Years later, she was in the audience at a Sitwell reading, but the encounter did not turn out quite as she may have hoped all those years earlier. Recognizing the now famous other literary lady, Sitwell refers to her as "that great poetess, Dorothy Wadden" (her contorted pronunciation of "Warren," thus making it a *double* accidental insult). Although Dame Edith had intended praise, the Parker reaction was anything but pleased— "Why, that Goddam Limey!"

Her breakthrough piece of verse—published in September 1914—was called "Any Porch" and introduced the conversational style of much of her mature work, with the story being conveyed in dialogue. A group of middle-class ladies sit around chatting, and we are left to picture them individually from what they say:

> I don't want the vote for myself,
> But women with property, dear—
> I think the poor girl's on the shelf,
> She's talking about her "career"

> I really look thinner, you say?
> I've lost all my hips? Oh, you're *sweet*—
> Imagine the city today!
> Humidity's *much* worse than heat!

When she was offered the job at *Vogue* in 1913, she told Crowninshield ("a lovely man but puzzled") that she had been reading fashion magazines "since I was a woman of twelve," but, she added, "fashion would never become a religion" with her. And as for the temple of that fashion—the excessively art-directed *Vogue* offices—"Well, it looks just like the entrance to a house of ill-fame."

"Funny, they were plain women working at *Vogue*, not chic. They were decent, nice women—the nicest women I ever met—but they had no business on such a magazine. They wore funny little bonnets and in the pages of their magazine they virginized the models from tough babes into exquisite little loves."

Edna Chase, the editor of *Vogue* at the time, remembered Dorothy as "a small dark-haired pixie, treacle-sweet of tongue but vinegar witted"—a verdict that her work in print certainly confirmed. Friends said of her that she spoke quietly with "a little drawl that was very attractive, very upper class."

She was set to work to write captions for the fashion illustrations:

"From these foundations of the Autumn wardrobe, one may learn that brevity is the soul of lingerie—as the Petticoat said to the Chemise."

"This little pink dress will win you a beau."

"Right *Dress*! For Milady's motor jaunt."

"Women need not be suppressed in order to be Stayed."

"There was a little girl who had a little curl, right in the middle of her forehead. When she was good she was very, very good, and when she was bad she wore this divine nightdress of rose-colored *mousseline de soie*, trimmed with frothy Valenciennes lace."

Ten dollars a week didn't give a working girl much financial leeway, and Dorothy Parker found herself a room "in a boarding house at 103rd and Broadway, paying eight dollars a week for my room and two meals, breakfast and dinner."

A fellow lodger was another aspiring writer, Thorne Smith (who was to write the Topper series of comic novels in the 1920s but was currently employed as an advertising copy-writer). The two of them had a brief affair, then settled down to a lifelong friendship. "We were both as poor as church mice; the kind that eat little but squeak a lot. . . . We used to sit around in the evening and talk. There was no money but, Jesus, we had fun."

For some time, in addition to her work at *Vogue*, she had been contributing verse to "The Conning Tower," a prestigious daily column edited by Franklin P. Adams in the *New York Tribune*. So prestigious was it that FPA (as he was universally known) never felt the need to pay his contributors. Nor did he choose to name them, so it is now impossible to identify Dorothy's early verses. Nonetheless, she was duly grateful for the honor and the experience it represented and always claimed that Adams—whom she was later to know well as a fellow member of the Algonquin Round Table—"raised me from a couplet."

In late 1917, Crowninshield moved her to *Vanity Fair*. Presumably she was given a raise, but, as she said in a line she was to use more than once, "Salary is no object. I want only enough to keep body and soul apart."

Vanity Fair in those days was a general-interest "up-market" magazine that looked at life and society with a slightly quizzical but generally uncritical gaze—a fact that gave its new recruit a problem from the outset. "[It] was a magazine of no opinions but *I* had opinions."

Most of those opinions—when they came to be expressed in literary form—turned out to be decidedly critical. During the three years she worked there, she continued to write a series of vers libre poems she had started to contribute while still at *Vogue*. She called them "Songs of Hate."

Her "hates" included men ("They irritate me"), relatives ("They cramp my style"), Bohemians ("They shatter my morale"), parties ("They bring out the worst in me"), college boys ("They get under my feet"), the younger set ("They harden my arteries"), wives ("Too many people have them"), and husbands ("They narrow my scope").

WOMEN

I hate women;
They get on my nerves.
. . .
And then there are those who are always in Trouble.
Always.
Usually they have Husband-trouble.
They are Wronged.
They are the women whom nobody—understands.
They wear faint, wistful smiles.
And when spoken to, they start.
They begin by saying they must suffer in silence.
No one will ever know—
And then they go into details.

RELATIVES

Then there are in-laws,
The Necessary Evils of Matrimony
The only things they don't say about you
Are the ones they can't pronounce.

ACTRESSES

There are the Adventuresses,
The Ladies with Lavender Pasts.
They wear gowns that show all their emotions,
And they simply can't stop undulating.
. . .
There are the Wronged Ones;
The Girls Whose Mothers Never Told Them.
In the first act they wear pink gingham and sunbonnets
And believe implicitly in the stork.
In the third act they are clad in somber black
And know that there isn't any Santa Claus.
. . .

Then there are the child Actresses
Who should be unseen and not heard.
They go around telling people about Heaven
As if they were special correspondents.

BOHEMIANS

Genius is an infinite capacity for giving pains.

HUSBANDS

And whenever you go out to have a good time,
You always meet them.

Another institution she claimed to hate was the office:

OUR OFFICE

I hate the Office;
It cuts in on my social life.

There is the Boss;
The Great White Chief.
He made us what we are today—
I hope he's satisfied.
He has some bizarre ideas
About his employees getting to work
At about nine o'clock in the morning—
As if they were a lot of milkmen.
He has never been known to see you
When you arrive at 8:45,
But try to come in at a quarter past ten
And he will always go up in the elevator with you.

Even then there was a certain sourness in her humor. It was "the laughter of disdain."

In a 1916 *Vogue* piece, "Why I Haven't Married," she would sat-irize various types of men who fell short of her standards, includ-ing (prophetically) the heavy drinker in whose affections she feared she would rate third—"first and second, Haig and Haig."

She had praise for only one archetype—"an English Greek God, just masterful enough to be entertaining. Just wicked enough to be exciting, just clever enough to be a good audience." Unfortunately, he had inadvertently married "a blonde and rounded person whose walk in life was upon the runway at the Winter Garden."

In real life, however, she married her Greek god—and changed her name. On June 30, 1917, she became the wife of Edwin Pond Parker II, of Hartford, Connecticut, a Wall Street stockbroker and the descendant of a well-to-do congressional clergy family, thus further stirring the interdenominational bouillabaisse.

Although later in life she would insist that she had mar-ried Eddie Parker mainly because he had "a nice, clean name," there is every reason to believe that she loved him at the time. Unfortunately for both of them, time was a commodity in short supply. Within days of the wedding, Eddie had enlisted and gone off to war. She had been a bride, she said, "for about five minutes."

One way and another, she found it increasingly difficult to keep satire out of her work. An article, "Interior Decoration," for instance, was submitted as "Interior Desecration"— the "creative" variation not being spotted until the piece was in print, much to the horror of the straight-laced Miss Chase. Throughout her career, editors learned to be wary and to look long and hard for the subversive subtext Mrs. Parker might have secreted between the lines.

Robert Benchley was to dub the Parker style the "Elevated Eyebrow School of Journalism," and "Mr. Benchley"—as she would always deferentially refer to him—was to become her clos-est friend and arbiter for the rest of his life.

Robert Benchley.

When Benchley was appointed managing editor of *Vanity Fair* in June 1919—having been a regular contributor for some time—Dorothy Parker found in him her ideal soul mate. Four years older than her and of a similarly irreverent turn of mind, he, too, could see the farce behind life's facades. She found his self-deprecating humor "a leaping of the mind," and the two of them in combination added up to far more than the sum of the parts, particularly when it came to creating mayhem.

When they shared an office, "Both Mr. Benchley and I subscribed to two undertaking magazines: *The Casket* and *Sunnyside*. Steel yourself. *Sunnyside* had a joke column called 'From Grave to Gay.' I cut a picture from one of them, in color, of how and where to inject embalming fluid, and had it hung over my desk until Mr. Crowninshield asked if I could possibly take it down. . . . We behaved extremely badly."

Before long, the duo became a trio, as Crowninshield hired a new drama editor, the six-foot-seven-inch war veteran Robert Sherwood. Whereas Benchley and Parker chattered nonstop, Sherwood was distinctly laconic. Parker claimed that he was a "Conversation Stopper" and that trying to talk to him was "like riding on the Long Island Railroad—it gets you nowhere in particular." Nonetheless, his silence was a friendly one, and he did wear his straw hat in rakish fashion, which she considered "pretty fast."

The three of them took to lunching together every day, and, to begin with, Benchley and Parker's function was to protect the elongated Sherwood ("a walking pipe organ") from being "attacked by the midgets" they might encounter en route.

The *Vanity Fair* offices on West 44th Street were quite close to the Hippodrome vaudeville theater, where a troupe of midgets were currently playing. When the three colleagues walked past, the midgets took great delight in making a beeline for Sherwood. "They were always sneaking up behind him and asking him how the weather was up there. . . . Mr. Benchley and I would leave our jobs and guide him down the street. I can't tell you, we had more fun." It took all the handling skills of the other two to coax their thoroughbred colleague along and into the safe haven of the nearby Algonquin Hotel, their customary watering hole.

And there, when the midgets had left town, began another tale entirely.

Inconstant Reviewer

"Ah," I said to myself, for I love a responsive audience,
"so it's one of those plays."

—*New Yorker* review

Scratch an actor . . . and you'll find an actress.

—Attributed

I hate Actors;
They ruin my evenings.

—"Actors: A Hymn of Hate"

I hate the Drama;
It cuts in on my sleep.

—"The Drama: A Hymn of Hate"

*It grieves me deeply to find out how frequently and
how violently wrong I can be—it doesn't seem reasonable, somehow.*

—Dorothy Parker

IN APRIL 1918, *Vanity Fair*'s resident drama critic, P. G.
Wodehouse, decided to take a European sabbatical, and
Dorothy Parker was designated to be his temporary replace-
ment. She was clearly conscious—to the point of being self-
conscious—about the singularity of her position as the only
woman in New York to hold such a position of influence and
sought to make light of it, often signing her pieces "Hélène
Rousseau." She was merely, she claimed ingenuously, "a tired
business woman . . . seeking innocent diversion."

In practice she created a new genre of dramatic criticism.
Instead of playing the traditional role of objective critic survey-
ing the scene from Mount Olympus, she rolled up her designer
sleeves and got down into the dust of the arena. Her critic was a
character in the drama she was reviewing, her writing style personal and colloquial. Not for the first time—and certainly not
for the last—she rejected the traditional concept of the "woman
writer" and substituted for it the feisty persona that was to
become her literary trademark and one that she would continue
to refine.

More often than not, she clearly didn't much care for what
she was required to see.

"Sometimes I think it can't be true . . . there couldn't be
plays as bad as these. In the first place, no one would write them,
and in the second place, no one would produce them . . . a long
succession of thin evenings. . . . It may be that a life of toil has
blunted my perception of the humorous."

In one case, she refused to name either the author or the
cast of a particular play. She said she was "not going to tell on
them."

Yes, occasionally she saw something that moved her.

"We bashfully admit that we wept, and lavishly; but on the other hand, it is but fair to admit that we are that way. All you have to do is drop a hat, and if we are in any kind of form we will break down and cry like a little tired child. . . . It is true that I paid it the tribute of tears, but that says nothing, for I am one who weeps at Victorian costumes. (I am also, for your files, one who cries at violincello renditions of 'Mighty Lak a Rose,' so you see.)"

The theatrical practitioners with whom she came in contact—both then and later—learned the hard way to beware of this demure-looking little woman with the quick tongue and the sharper pen. They should have been warned by her "Hate Songs," particularly those relating to the stage:

I hate Actresses;
They get on my nerves.

"In the first act the heroine is strangled by one of her admirers," she wrote in a *New Yorker* review. "For me, the murder came too late."

And many a famous actress came to grief in the limpid depths of her innocent gaze and sweet delivery when the two of them met in person.

Kitty Carlisle Hart (or in some versions Katharine Cornell) was once inveigled into telling Mrs. Parker of her early days behind the footlights. "And there I was in the Capitol theatre at 10:30 in the morning, walking out on a stage for the first

THE ACTRESS'S TOMBSTONE

Her name, cut clear upon this marble cross,
Shines, as it shone when she was still on earth;
While tenderly the mild agreeable moss
Obscures the figures of her date of birth.

("Tombstones in the Starlight")

time in my life to face thirty-six hundred people." To which her open-mouthed audience replied, "They made you do *that*? Oh, you poor *child*! That *huge* place, and all those people out front *staring* at you, waiting to *devour* you! Just to think of it makes my heart *ache*! You dear, brave *Baby*!" She got away with quite a lot of this before the object of her "sympathy" caught on that she was being spoon-fed molasses. This remark pales beside her notorious verdict on Katharine Hepburn's performance in *The Lake*, that "Miss Hepburn runs the gamut of emotion from A to B"—a verdict with which Miss Hepburn was subsequently inclined to agree. "I'm sure I gave a *foul* performance—chaotic."

Parker rubbed salt deeper into the wound by observing that Miss Hepburn took care to keep away from one of the supporting actresses, "in case she caught acting from her." In point of fact, Parker greatly admired Hepburn as an actress. When Garson Kanin asked her years later whether she had been misquoted, she replied, "Oh, I said it all right. You know how it is. A joke. When people expect you to say things, you say things. Isn't that the way it is?"

And that's almost certainly the way it was with many of her remarks. People did come to expect them from Dorothy Parker—and they were rarely disappointed.

The reviews for *Vanity Fair* helped her sharpen her pen and cut a few legends down to what she considered the appropriate size. In a revival of *Hedda Gabler*, it was "the shot that marked [Nazimova's] spectacular final exit" that caught her ear.

"Shots almost always do mark the final exit of Mr. Ibsen's heroines. I do wish that he had occasionally let the ladies take bichloride of mercury, or turn on the gas, or do something quiet and neat around the house. I invariably miss most of the lines in the last act of an Ibsen play; I always have my fingers in my ears, waiting for the loud report that means that the heroine has just Passed On."

Despite her reservations, she counted Ibsen—along with Chekhov and Shaw—as her favorite playwrights.

There was also the echo of live ammunition from the war in Europe—a subject that produced a plethora of "war plays." "I have had so much propaganda poured into me that I couldn't hold another drop. I have witnessed so many German spies that I have begun to distrust my own family."

Tolstoy's *Redemption* did little to lift her spirits.

"It isn't what you would call sunny. I went into the Plymouth Theatre a comparatively young woman, and I staggered out of it, three hours later, twenty years older, haggard and broken with suffering. . . .

"It is difficult to speak of 'atmosphere' and 'feeling' without sounding as if one wore sandals and lived below Fourteenth Street. . . .

"I do wish they would do something about those Russian names. Owing to the custom of calling each person sometimes by all of his names, sometimes only by his first three or four, and sometimes by a nickname which has nothing to do with any of the other names, it is difficult for someone with my congenital lowness of brow to gather exactly who they are talking about. I do wish that, as long as they are translating the thing, they would go right ahead, while they're at it, and translate Fedor Vasilyevich Protosov and Sergei Dmitrievich Abreskov and Ivan Petrovich Alexandrovic into Joe and Harry and Fred."

A particular bête noir was the tendency of contemporary middle-class playwrights to "write down" when dealing with the lower classes.

"The sentimental passages seemed to leave me cold. Because a young woman says 'H'aint' and 'you was' and admits that she 'don't know nothin' about art,' doesn't seem to me to be any particular reason for a man to clasp her passionately in his arms and tell her that she is a wild, sweet, fairy thing—a creature of the spring woods" (about *Tiger! Tiger!* by Edward Knoblock).

"To begin with, *Tillie* is a dialect play—and, so far as I am concerned, it's to end with too."

Occasionally the fare on offer would bring on a temporary hysteria of the pen—as with Sem Benelli's *The Jest*.

"Without wishing to infringe in any way on the Pollyanna copyright, there are times when one must say a few kind words for the general scheme of things. When things have sunk to their lowest depths, some really desirable event occurs. . . . When clouds are thickest, the sun is due to come out strong in a little while. In fact, the darkest hour is just before the dawn (No originality is claimed for that last one; it is just brought in for the heart interest and popular appeal)."

Of another play, she wrote: "The scene is laid in France, thus giving each member of the cast an opportunity to pronounce the word 'Monsieur' in a different way. . . .

"But then, as the optimistic woman who left the theatre just a little way in front of me, observed, 'Well, it's a clean show, anyway.'"

Dotty's first drama stint—as will be seen—ended rather abruptly in 1920, but in 1931 she was back in her aisle seat, filling in this time for Robert Benchley. As Alexander Woollcott put it, "It would be her idea of her duty to catch up the torch as it fell from his hand—and burn someone with it." Absence had not staled the infinite variety of her wit one whit.

In *The Barretts of Wimpole Street*, she found Katharine Cornell "a completely lovely Elizabeth Barrett . . . [she] displays the beautiful, clean angle from the tip of her chin to the hollow of her throat to the audience. Her voice is more thrilling than ever, so that it is perhaps cavilling to say that, thrilling though the music may be, it would be nice, now and then, to distinguish some of the words. Perhaps cavilling it is, but here I am saying it.

"Now that you've got me right down to it, the only thing I didn't like about *The Barretts of Wimpole Street* was the play (Personal: Robert Benchley, please come home. Nothing is forgiven.)"

Things failed to improve with A. A. Milne's *Give Me Yesterday*: "Its hero is caused by a novel device to fall asleep and a-dream; and thus he is given yesterday. Me, I should have given him twenty years to life. . . .

"In a shifting, sliding world, it is something to know that Mr. A. A. ("Whimsy-the-Pooh") Milne stands steady. . . . If *Give Me Yesterday* is a fine play, I am Richard Brinsley Sheridan (Personal: Robert Benchley, please come home. Whimso is back again.)"

Mrs. Parker had a rooted aversion to Milne in all his pastel moods and a little history to go with it. In 1928 she had been required—in her capacity as "Constant Reader"—to review his latest offering, a book called *The House at Pooh Corner*, in which Piglet asks Pooh why he has added the phrase "Tiddely-pom" to a song, and Pooh answers, "To make it more hummy."

"And it is that word 'hummy,' my darlings, that marks the first place in *The House at Pooh Corner* at which Tonstant Weader fwowed up."

She even went so far as to pen some "Lines on discovering that you have been advertised as America's A. A. Milne." To her it was the ultimate insult:

WHEN WE WERE VERY SORE

Dotty had
Great Big
Visions of
Quietude.
Dotty saw an
Ad, and it
Left her
Flat.
Dotty had a
Great Big
Snifter of
Cyanide.
And that (said Dotty)
Is that.

No play or performer was safe.

She could not keep silent about 1931's *The Silent Witness*: "[Kay Strozzi] had the temerity to wear as truly horrible a gown as ever I have seen on the American stage. There was a flowing skirt of pale chiffon—you men don't have to listen—and a bodice of rose-coloured taffeta, the sleeves of which ended shortly below her shoulders. Then there was an expanse of naked arms, and then, around the wrists, taffeta frills such as are fastened about the unfortunate necks of beaten white poodle-dogs in animal acts. Had she not been strangled by a member of the cast while disporting this garment, I should have fought my way to the stage and done her in, myself."

According to Parker, the husband of French actress Jeanne Aubert, "if you can believe the papers, recently pled through the French courts that he be allowed to restrain his wife from appearing on the stage. Professional or not, the man is a dramatic critic."

Reviewing Channing Pollock's 1933 offering *The House Beautiful*: "*The House Beautiful* is the play lousy." Nor should the *audience* feel too secure. At a performance of (Pierre) Louÿs's *Aphrodite*: "There is even a brand-new drop-curtain for the occasion, painted with the mystic letters (ΑΦΡΟΔΙΤΗ) which most of the audience take to be the Greek word for 'asbestos.'"

But eventually, like all sentences, it was over, and on April 11, 1931, she could write, "This is a fairly solemn moment. Here I am, taking my formal leave of the New York theatre, before I go, free, white and eighty-one, out to battle with the larger and, I can but hope, the kindlier world.

"Goodbyes are best said briefest. So I thank you all so very much and, though I certainly had a rotten time, I hate to leave you."

It was not the first time she had taken her leave—simply the first she had taken voluntarily.

In January 1920, Crowninshield had fired her from *Vanity Fair* ("Since that time," she reported more than forty years later,

"I've been freelancing"). "I fixed three plays . . . and as a result I was fired. . . . The plays closed and the producers, who were very big boys—Dillingham (*Apple Blossom*), Ziegfeld (*Caesar's Wife*) and Belasco (*The Son-Daughter*)—didn't like it, you know. . . . So I was fired."

The final nail in her critical coffin was her verdict on the performance of Billie Burke, the current Mrs. Ziegfeld: "In her desire to convey the girlishness of the character, she plays her lighter scenes as if she were giving an impersonation of Eva Tanguay." And since Miss Tanguay was a well-known burlesque performer and was most definitely *not* to be considered a serious actress, Miss Burke was not amused. Nor, when Ziegfeld had threatened to remove his considerable advertising, was Condé Nast.

Exit Dorothy Parker stage left.

On hearing the news, "Mr. Benchley and Mr. Sherwood resigned their jobs." Sherwood was a free agent, but Benchley's decision surprised her. "Mr. Benchley had a family—two children. It was the greatest act of friendship I'd known."

When they had cleared their desks, Mr. Benchley and Mrs. Parker rented a tiny office ("an over-sized broom closet") over the Metropolitan Opera House studios near Times Square for thirty dollars a month. "One cubic foot less of space," Benchley claimed, "and it would have constituted adultery."

But the legends at least grew. They applied for the cable address "Parkbench." They put up a sign that read, "The Utica Drop Forge and Tool Company. Benchley and Parker—Presidents." And after Benchley's departure for a job at *Life*, Mrs. Parker wrote "Men" on the door so as to see new faces.

None of these appear to have been true, though they made good and often-repeated stories, and Parker did write to a friend in her Hollywood days threatening to display that very same legend on her studio office door. She was then and was to remain a magnet for the iron filings of every memorable line or anecdote. "It got so bad that they began to laugh before I opened my mouth."

During their brief "partnership," they made desultory attempts at various literary ventures, including a play. But all of them evaporated in laughter and lunch.

By midyear, both of them were writing for *Life* with Parker contributing to a column called "The Far-Sighted Muse" as well as selling articles to the *Saturday Evening Post.* She gave up her Men's Room.

Since change was clearly in the air, she also moved to a new apartment. A real estate agent showed her one that was far removed from the modest dwelling she had in mind. "Oh, dear, that's *much* too big. All I need is room to lay a hat and a few friends." Another was "far enough East to plant tea." She finally found what she required on West 57th Street.

"I was making good money but as far as a 'few million' went. . . . I figure, by the way things are running now," she wrote, "I ought to have it piled up somewhere around the late spring of 2651."

She and Benchley were not proud; they wrote advertising copy for clients like Stetson hats.

"I don't say that I am one of those big business women that make anywhere between ten and twelve dollars a month, in their spare time, by reading character from the shape of the hair-cut or the relative positions of the mouth and the ear. In fact, if I were to sit down and tell you how often I have been fooled on some of the most popular facial characteristics, I'd be here all afternoon. All I say is, give me a good, honest look at a man's hat and the way he wears it, and I'll tell you what he is within five pounds, or give you your money back."

There had to be more to the life literary than this. And there was.

Queen Dorothy and the Round Table

The greatest collection of unsaleable wit in America.

—Herman Manckiewicz

Damn it, it was the twenties and we had to be smarty. . . . I think the trouble with us was that we stayed too young.

—Dorothy Parker

It was no Mermaid Tavern, I can tell you. Just a bunch of loudmouths showing off. . . . The whole thing was made up by people who'd never been there. And may I say they're still making it up?

—Dorothy Parker recalling the
Algonquin Round Table in the 1950s

A Vicious Circle by Natalie Ascensios, a mural in the dining room (The Round Table Room) at the Algonquin Hotel. *Back row:* Robert Benchley, The Algonquin Cat, Robert Sherwood, Harpo Marx, Alexander Woollcott, Marc Connelly, Edna Ferber. *Front row:* Dorothy Parker, Frank Case, Harold Ross, George S. Kaufman, Heywood Broun.

THE HOTEL LOBBY in which Benchley, Parker, and Sherwood sought refuge from the midgets had begun life in 1902 as a temperance hotel, appropriately named The Puritan. Fortunately, those days were long gone. It was now the Algonquin, and it would have been happy to serve liquor had not the Volstead Act of 1919 made that illegal. But Prohibition was just about the only prohibition. Frank Case—who managed it from the outset and later owned it—named it after that particular Indian tribe because, according to his research, they were the first and strongest people known to have lived in that neighborhood.

Funds being low as usual, the trio made their lunch from the substantial hors d'oeuvres on offer or scrambled eggs and coffee. Case had prudently decided that one quick way to raise the profile of his establishment was to attract a coterie of promising (if currently impecunious) literary folk from the many magazines and newspapers that had offices in the immediate vicinity—and the tactic appeared to be working.

Shrewdly, he caught the tide of a generation of young writers returning from the war and seeking to establish themselves—not to mention justify themselves and what they had contributed to the recent conflict. One such was Alexander Woollcott—a burly, soon-to-be-gargantuan journalist at the *New York Times*—who was given a dinner at the Algonquin in his honor on his return from the war. The occasion allowed him to tell endless stories which began, "When I was in the theatre of war . . ." Delighted with the evening, he is supposed to have suggested to the assembled guests, "Why don't we do this *every* day?," which the core group somehow drifted into doing.

Dorothy Parker saw this orgy of self-congratulation with a rather more jaundiced eye than most and wrote (in a 1919 *Vanity Fair* article under the pen name "Helen Wells") about "the numerous heroes who nobly accepted commissions in those branches of the services where the fountain pen is mightier than the sword." She referred to them as "the Fountain Pen Lancers" or the "Fireside Hussars" and was to lament "the fact that my

Alexander Woollcott as sketched by William Auerbach-Levy.

husband went to the front—it made him seem like such a slacker. And then to think that all this fuss has been made about the men in France, when the war was won right back home all the time."

It was not the first sign of her disillusionment she had expressed at the ballyhoo that had accompanied her country's belated commitment to the conflict. In *Vanity Fair* in 1918, she wrote:

"You know, there's something gravely wrong with me. I have just realized it lately. I never knew I was unpatriotic before—I'm the wife of one of Our Boys and I wasn't wild about the Germans long before this war ever started. But there is something seriously the matter—I simply cannot get all worked up at the sight of a company of chorus men clad in uniforms, even though they march up to the very footlights with a do-or-die expression in their eyes. If this be treason, make the most of it."

And then there were those patriotic women who insisted on entertaining the soldiers on leave with "songs of such cheerful sentiments as 'You May Be Gone For A Long, Long Time' and 'When You Come Back—If You Do Come Back.' They have also memorized scores of ballads in which soldier sons are perpetually bidding farewell to Mother—those songs in which the lyricist has the unparalleled opportunity of rhyming 'mother' with 'love her' and 'soldier' with 'shoulder.' "

When the lunches began to become a regular feature of the Algonquin's daily life—starting approximately in June 1919—Case put the group in the Pergola (now the Oak) Room and gave them a long table. They began to refer to themselves as the Luigi Board—after all, their dictatorial waiter was called Luigi, and the Ouija Board was in fashion. This soon became "The Board," and they launched their "Board meetings." By virtue of where the table was placed, the group faced a mirrored wall so that as their numbers increased, they actually multiplied. Case then moved them to the front of the main Rose Room and gave them a round table. Thus was the "Round Table" and the "Vicious Circle" born.

In later years, Dorothy Parker was highly ambivalent about the phenomenon she had helped create. There were times when she would actually deny having been there.

"Mr. Benchley and I weren't there for the simple reason that we couldn't afford it. It cost money and we weren't just poor, we were penniless."

All the evidence, of course, is otherwise, and in later years she was prone to exaggerate. Nonetheless, in retrospect, she was consistently critical. In a January 1959 television interview:

"People romanticize it. It was no Mermaid Tavern, I promise you. These weren't giants. Think of who was writing in those days—Lardner, Fitzgerald, Faulkner and Hemingway. Those were the real giants. The Round Table was just a lot of people telling jokes and telling each other how good they were. Just a bunch of loudmouths showing off, saving their gags for days, waiting for a chance to spring them. 'Did you hear about my remark?' 'Did I tell you what I said?' and everybody banging around saying, 'What'd he say?' It wasn't legendary. I don't mean that—but it wasn't all that good. There was no truth in anything they said. It was the terrible day of the wisecracks, so there didn't have to be any truth, you know. There's nothing memorable about them. About any of them. . . .

"At first, I was in awe of them because they were being published. But then I came to realize I wasn't hearing anything very stimulating. I remember hearing Woollcott say, 'Reading Proust is like lying in somebody else's dirty bath water.' And then he'd go into ecstasy about something called *Valiant is the Word for Carrie*, and I knew I'd had enough of the Round Table."

She would add unkindly and untruthfully, "Most of them hadn't read anything written before 1920. Most of them are dead now, but they weren't too alive then."

And what of the Ladies of the Round Table—actress Peggy Wood, writers Edna Ferber and Alice Duer Miller, journalists Jane Grant and Ruth Hale, Tallulah Bankhead ("Whistler's Mother"), and others?

"We were gallant, hard-riding and careless of life. We were little black ewes that had gone astray; we were a sort of Ladies' Auxiliary of the Legion of the Damned. And, boy, were we proud of our shame! When Gertrude Stein spoke of a 'Lost Generation,' we took it to ourselves and considered it the prettiest compliment we had."

As far as the group—and, indeed, their whole generation—was concerned, "The whole point of their lives was to have fun, to be clever, to know where the best bartenders were, to be knowledgeable about the city, to know all the latest catchwords, to be aware of the latest fads and fashions, to go to all the first nights, to be satirical and blasé and to do as little work as possible."

Anita Loos had the Round Tablers in mind when in *Gentlemen Prefer Blondes* she has her heroine, Lorelei Lee, observe that they were "so busy thinking up some cute remark to make that they never have time to do any listening."

Alexander Woollcott and Edna Ferber as sketched by James Montgomery Flagg.

Seen in retrospect, it was an almost inevitable reaction on the part of a generation that had survived the "war to end all wars" and found itself in a time of social and economic flux in which all previously accepted values were in doubt in a society they firmly believed to be rotten. It was not that Dorothy Parker and her set were in active revolt against that society—they merely felt superior to it and considered it irrelevant. They refused to be bound by its rules.

"Silly of me to blame it on dates," she told a 1958 interviewer, "but so it happened to be. Dammit, it was the Twenties and we *had* to be smart. I *wanted* to be cute. That's the terrible thing. I should have had more sense. I was the toast of two continents: Greenland and Australia."

But she would also dub the 1920s "The Dingy Decade."

Screenwriter Herman Manckiewicz (later to inspire Orson Welles to *Citizen Kane*), an occasional Round Tabler himself, was uncomfortably close to the mark when he dubbed his fellow lunchers as "the greatest collection of unsaleable wit in America."

Even so, most of them were published regularly, if only by each other. So FPA would describe the doings and sayings of Woollcott, Parker, Benchley, Kaufman, Heywood Broun, Ring Lardner, and others—then Woollcott and Broun would return the favor. "Logrolling" was the phrase used to describe the self-congratulatory and self-fulfilling process. The "Algonks" were early examples of the "celebrity"—well known for being famous and famous for being well known. They were an interesting but ill-assorted bunch.

There was the epicene Alexander Woollcott, drama critic, journalist, and the self-elected leader of the pack. He was basically

Harpo Marx would often turn up at the Round Table—and he was rarely silent!

afraid of Parker and her quick tongue, which made for a durable relationship between the two of them. On one occasion he was describing his latest book signing. "After all, what is so rare as a Woollcott first edition?" he asked rhetorically. "A *second* edition."

She liked him enough to think up a pet name for his new apartment on the East River. Having originally called it "Old Manse River," she finally settled on "Wit's End." He became, she would write, "as close to essential as one friend can be to another."

Nonetheless, she was well aware of his limitations and considered his literary pretensions "ridiculous." "He had a good heart, for whatever that was worth, and it wasn't much." He in his turn declared that she was "an odd blend of Little Nell and Lady Macbeth."

Another returned war correspondent to sit around the Table was the unlikely Harold Ross. Parker was initially dismissive of a man she found to be "almost illiterate, wild and rough . . . a monolith of unsophistication" who had "never read anything and didn't know anything." She was as surprised as anyone when in 1925 he actually did what he had long been *talking* of doing and founded a magazine—*The New Yorker*—which was to give legitimacy, not to mention employment, to the incessant talkers and occasional writers from the Algonquin.

As for the rest, in her view, "[H. L.] Mencken was impossible. . . . FPA was a lovely man, disagreeable and rude—but lovely. . . . George Kaufman was a mess . . . a worker in mosaics. . . . So much kudos for so little talent . . . I see nothing in that talent at all. . . . Oh, I suppose I do, but you know what I mean . . . [critic George Jean] Nathan is missed. None of the others are. . . . It's just that there was so much praise."

She was careful to exempt her old silent sparring partner, Robert Sherwood, who would go on to be one of his generation's leading playwrights (*Idiot's Delight, The Petrified Forest, Reunion in Vienna*). Having delivered him from the midgets, she would cable him when she felt he had absented himself too long from the Round Table: "We've turned down a vacant stepladder for you."

As a group, they found themselves locked in intellectual incest—"the game the whole family can play," as any one of them might have written—and became very sensitive when it seemed appropriate to each other's work.

"You might set fire to widows, deflower orphans, or filch the flag from soldier's graves and still be invited to all the literary teas; but if you admired in print, the traits and achievements of any member of your acquaintance, your jig was up. . . . The fear of becoming a log-roller was put into me during my formative years, and there was a good long stretch during which, in my endeavors to keep clean of the ugly charge, I said only the vilest of my nearest and dearest."

Indeed, there were moments—many of them—of literate gaiety. For instance, there was The Game. You had to take the multisyllabic word you were given and turn it into a pun within ten seconds. It was a pastime at which Dorothy Parker reigned supreme:

> HORTICULTURE: "You can lead a horticulture but you can't make her think."
> BURLESQUE: "I had soft burlesques for breakfast."
> PENIS: "The penis mightier than the sword."

And it only got worse:

> LAITY: "Laity of Spain, I adore you."
> HIAWATHA: "Hiawatha nice girl till I met you."
> "Do you know the celery song?" "Celery gather at the river?"
> The Irish song? "Irish I was in Dixie."
> The French song? "Je suis have no bananas."
> The Spanish national anthem? "José, can you see?"
> Paris was a "Paroxysmarvelous city."
> GARTER: "Nearer my garter to thee."

"They were all living lives of extreme casualness," Dr. Alvan Baruch notes as early as 1924, when he had several of the

Algonks as his patients. "Nearly all of them had a terrible malicious streak." He sensed that most of them had a strong suspicion they were skating on perilously thin professional ice.

The Wall Street crash of 1929 brought the 1920s to an ignominious end in all sorts of ways, and it took the Round Table with it. Many of them lost heavily, though fortunately Dorothy Parker was not one of them. "I never had the sophistication to play the market."

In a late story, she caught the atmosphere of the time all too well:

"It was a year when there were many along the sidewalks mouthing soliloquies, and unless they talked loud and made gestures other pedestrians did not turn to look."

In 1933, Frank Case tried to revive the spirit of the Round Table by setting up an Algonquin Supper Club—but the moment had passed. By 1938, for him, it had faded into "a pleasant and mellow memory." The same year also saw the death of the first of the Algonks: Ring Lardner. One by one they went, leaving footprints of varying depths to show they had passed this way—Heywood Broun in 1939, Woollcott in 1943, Benchley in 1945, Ross in 1951, Sherwood in 1955, FPA in 1960, and Kaufman in 1961. ("So many of them died. My Lord, how people die!")

Ironically, Dorothy Parker, who had always toyed with death, outlived them all.

CHAPTER

5

Hi-Ho-Hum Society

As only New Yorkers know, if you can get through the twilight, you'll live through the night.

—"New York at 6:30 p.m."

At my birth the Devil touched my tongue.

—Dorothy Parker

I'm the greatest little runner-down there ever was.

—Dorothy Parker

The steps in social ascent may be gauged by the terms employed to describe a man's informal evening dress: the progression goes tuxedo, Tux, dinner jacket, Black Tie.

—"The Game"

41

ROBERT BENCHLEY once impressed—and depressed—
Dorothy Parker by his gloomy prediction that each of
us is doomed to become the thing we most fear. Parker
feared two things—being considered a "woman writer" and turning into a "society lady." That fabrication she saw all too much
of in both her personal and her professional life, which was
replete with "over-eager portrait-painters, playwrights of dubi-
ous sexes, professional conversationalists, and society ladies not
quite divorced." Collaboration with Crowninshield on a book
called *High Society* during her *Vanity Fair* years merely confirmed
her right to be concerned.

There were so many social traps for the unwary. Language
was one of them:

INVICTUS

Farthest am I from perfection's heights,
Faulty am I as I well could be,
Still I insist on my share of rights.
When I am dead, think this of me:
Though I have uttered the words "Yea, bo."
Though I use "ain't" to get a laugh,
Though I am wont to exclaim "Let's go,"
Though I say "You don't know the half"—
Black though my record as darkest jet,
Give me, I beg, the devil's due;
Only remember I've never yet
Said, "How's the world been treating you?"

And it wasn't just *what* you said but how you *said* it:

"The sublimest thoughts in the English language can be
reduced to utter idiocy by pronouncing them with Southern
accent. Ah stray-ut lion is the shoat-ess distance between two
points, d'ya heah?"

Her pronunciational prejudice was hardened by her expo-
sure to the mother of Alan Campbell, her second husband, and

hence her temporary mother-in-law. "Mother Hortense . . . exudes that particular odour of Djer Kiss face powder and dried perspiration that characterizes the Southern gentlewoman. She is the only woman I know who pronounced the word 'egg' with three syllables."

Parker herself was pithy in any verbal medium. Like Noël Coward, she was a great believer in the terse vocabulary of the cablegram. When two of her friends who had been living together finally decided to marry, she wired her congratulations: "WHAT'S NEW?" And when Sherwood's wife, Mary, finally had a baby whose arrival she had talked about endlessly, Parker cabled, "DEAR MARY, WE ALL KNEW YOU HAD IT IN YOU."

BARTENDER: What are you having?

MRS. PARKER: Not much fun.

The Sherwood/Brandon wedding, October 1922. *Back row:* Robert Sherwood (*extreme left*); Robert Benchley (*second left*); Alexander Woollcott (*back turned*); Front row: Douglas Fairbanks (*extreme right*).

The social event was something that produced a permanent ambivalence. She couldn't bear *not* to go, yet she hated it when she was actually there. It's no accident that so many of her stories deal with social embarrassment of one kind or another.

By the time she joined the Round Table, Parker was already well known as a wit and someone whom party guests would pick out immediately. Invariably, many of them would seek to engage her in conversation so that they could take home some tidbit—"You'll never guess what she *said* . . ." only to discover that the encounter was not without risk.

Typical was the woman who simply asked, "Are you Dorothy Parker?" "Yes, do you mind?"

Yet this woman got off lightly compared with many others. There was the young man who took her to a party as his date. Trying to appear sophisticated, he looked at the revelry and affected to be bored by it. "I'm afraid I can't join in the merriment. I can't bear fools." "That's queer. Your mother could."

An aging lady seated near to her at dinner starts to ogle an Army colonel opposite. "It's his uniform. I just *love* soldiers," she unwisely confides to Parker. "Yes, you have in every war."

A female neighbor is agonizing about a small scratch she has received on her face—*not*, it should be added, from Mrs. Parker—"Oh, I *do* hope there won't be a scar." "As opposed to all those women who *like* looking as if they went to school in Heidelberg?"

Occasionally, the cracks could be almost benevolent, as when a man bent to retrieve her cigarette lighter and his knee joints cracked, "Ah, there's nothing like an open fire!"

But when you really had to worry was what the lady might say when you had to leave the group. When one man who was clearly ill at ease in the company excused himself to go to the men's room, Parker explained sweetly, "He *really* needs to telephone, but he's too embarrassed to say so."

Like everyone professional who deals in words—from the novelist to the stand-up comic—she was never averse to repeating a winning line, and at least once she used the routine to excuse herself.

Even a harmless parlor game was not necessarily safe. Playing Twenty Questions with some friends, she guessed that they were trying to identify a mutual acquaintance. "Would he be the kind of man who would put the wings back on flies?"

When she was on public show, she seemed to feel she must give her "public" their money's worth, and it brought out her more shocking one-liners. Was she enjoying the party? "*Enjoying* it? One more drink and I'll be under the host." Where do all these people come from? "When it's all over they crawl back into the woodwork."

In her last years, she mellowed to a degree, but the edge was still there. At the last formal dinner party she attended, her hostess, Gloria Vanderbilt, was expressing justifiable pride in her crystal wine glasses. "Oh, yes," Mrs. Parker politely agreed, "paper cups really wouldn't do."

But ironically, perhaps the truest accounts of her real feelings about such occasions are to be found in her fiction:

"Everyone else at the table had got up to dance, except him and me. There I was trapped. Trapped like a trap in a trap" ("The Waltz").

"I should have stayed at home for dinner. I could have had something on a tray. The head of John the Baptist, or something" ("But the One on the Right").

And should you have her as a weekend house guest, which many people did—at least once—you would always be wondering what she *really* thought behind that demure little smile and quiet little voice.

Woollcott recalled a weekend they were both guests at a friend's house and went to inspect the washing facilities. In the bathroom they were to share an ancient toothbrush had been left behind. "What do you suppose she does with it?" Woollcott asked her. "I think she rides it on Halloween."

On at least one occasion, though, her host did discover the truth. A house guest of *Saturday Evening Post* publisher George Lorrimer—a regular patron of the Parker output—she asked her host for permission to send a cable to Benchley. It read,

STELLA: You're strange people, if you are people. Strange and fascinating. You dismiss so much. . . . You sneer at the world, and yet you want to take it over. You slide over it like a film of ice. And where you've passed, nothing will grow.

(*The Ice Age*)

GORDON: You know, I would doubt if he is one.

DAISY: Look, there are people who think a man is that way if he speaks correct English.

(*The Ice Age*)

"PLEASE SEND ME A LOAF OF BREAD AND DON'T FORGET TO INCLUDE A SAW AND FILE."

Lorrimer happened to have the text read back to him for verification by the cable office, and she was never invited again, although he continued to publish her work.

Almost from the beginning, the gay community found an affinity for Dorothy Parker. As one of them said, they felt that they could "let their hair down" with her. She accepted the tribute, but her own feelings on the subject were mixed. When a number of them rallied around her after some particularly depressing love affair had ended, she explained to her Round Table colleagues that she needed "some good fairies to look after me."

For most of the time, though, they could expect to be treated precisely like everyone else—dismissively. When a young gay in a Greenwich Village bar asked her if she ever read fairy tales, she replied, "My dear, let us not talk shop."

And arriving at a party where she found herself surrounded by cross-dressing transsexuals and probably the only woman present, she leaned over the balcony and shouted to the assembled guests, "Come on up, anybody. I'm a *man*!"

Not that her own sex escaped scot-free when they crossed the line. When a group of lesbians in Paris were debating the possibility of legal same-sex marriage, Parker said, "Of course you must have legal marriages. The children have to be considered."

"Our language is so dexterous, let us call them ambi-sexterous"
"A Musical Comedy Thought"

Political correctness was not—and never would have been—a concept in the Parker canon. Her irreverence was totally asexual or possibly pansexual. When she was told that Christine Jorgenson—the first celebrity sex-change subject—was coming over to the United States to visit "her" mother, she enquired, "And what sex, may I ask, is the mother?"

And, of course, there was her notorious put-down of the young debutantes at the Yale prom, witnessed by Woollcott: "If all those sweet young things were laid end to end, I wouldn't be a bit surprised."

The Parker style was rarely the sculpted Wildean epigram, though she would no doubt have given much to have come up with some of his off-the-cuff replies:

If, with the literate, I am
Impelled to try an epigram,
I never seek to take the credit;
We all assume that Oscar said it.

ZABEL: After all, civilisation is the avoidance of disappointment, isn't it?

GORDON: Sounds like Oscar Wilde.

ZABEL: Oh, Wilde. Take the word nowadays away from Wilde and there would be very few epigrams left.

(The Ice Age)

She preferred to specialize in the verbal "counterpunch." When Arnold Gingrich, the publisher of *Esquire*, once remarked disingenuously at a party that he was just a simple country boy from Michigan, she was heard to add, "When convenient."

And when Mr. Benchley informed her that ex-President Coolidge had died, she asked innocently, "How could they tell?" (This is the commonly told version of the story, but Benchley's grandson Peter claims that he has his mother's word that Benchley then answered her, "He had an erection.")

When she said of a particular fellow guest, "You know, that woman speaks eighteen languages? And she can't say no in any of them," that may well have been a line waiting for its moment of delivery. But a great many of the best Parker ripostes had, by circumstance, to have been spontaneous.

Told by a friend that their hostess was outspoken—"By whom?" On an actress who had broken her leg in London—"Oh, how terrible. She must have done it sliding down a barrister." Or when she approached a taxi in the street only to be told, "I'm engaged"—"Then be happy."

She was clever but not publicly vulgar, so there are almost certainly lines attributed to her that she did *not* say. For example, Harold Ross, her editor on *The New Yorker*, is supposed to have phoned her when she was on her honeymoon with Alan Campbell, asking about a piece that was overdue. "Tell him I've been too fucking busy—or vice versa" seems a little obvious as a response for someone who was capable of saying at a Halloween party, when told that the guests were busy ducking for apples, "There, but for a typographical error, is the story of my life."

What she was perfectly capable of saying, though, was barbed enough. A certain lady was described as looking like "a two dollar whore who once commanded five," and when her attention was called to a woman wearing a cape trimmed with monkey fur—"Really? I thought they were beards." It was a process that her friend Lillian Hellman described as "embrace and denounce." To someone's face, she was all sweetness and light, but once they had departed . . .

When they entertained in Hollywood, she would stand beside Alan Campbell "reaching out my arms in my well-known gesture of welcome": . . . "Oh, how marvellous it is to see you again . . . do you want to meet any of the shits in here?" Of course, once you went in, you were, by definition, one of them.

A friend once asked Parker to stop running down a recently departed guest. She was a nice person who wouldn't hurt a fly. "Not if it was buttoned up," Parker couldn't help but reply.

She had—she claimed at one point—a friend "who is trying to make a lady of me, and the first step in the uphill climb has been the gaining of my promise to keep from employing certain words." The second step is unrecorded. The fact of the matter was that she could never suffer fools, gladly or otherwise—and her definition was a catholic one: "I cannot keep my face shut [but] as God hears me, I am perfectly justified."

Most of her stories dealt with the nuances of social behavior, quite often with "the gilt and brass of a certain type of American personality, the self-obsessed female snob." But she could skewer any member of her own sex with a verbal hat pin:

"She smiled heartily, waved her hand like a dear little baby shaking bye-bye, and schottisched across the floor to resume the burdens of hospitality."

"She is as deep as a dime, as profound as a work by Elinor Glyn, as receptive as a closed vault, as immediate as a topical song. She is, many people say, the perfect New York type."

"A streamline model lady (the wife of a prominent asphalt contractor) from the Palisade View Apartments in West 127th Street, sinking upon a heap of cushions and wondering if she really does look like Scheherezade, is indeed a sight to pluck at the heart-strings."

"Ladies with a genius for interpretive dancing have even gone to the trouble of bringing costumes. It is difficult to detect any difference between their costumes and their everyday attire. The way to tell is by glancing, as if casually, at their toes. If their feet are bare—they are performing."

"Mrs. Ernest Weldon wandered about the orderly living-room, giving it some of those little feminine touches. She was not especially good as a touch-giver . . . touch giving was a wife's job, and Mrs. Weldon was not one to shirk the business she had entered."

" 'Mr. Matson', she continued—she always spoke of her husband thus; it conveyed an aristocratic sense of aloofness, did away with any suggestion of carnal intimacy between them."

"For winter, she chose frocks of audible taffeta, frilled and frilled again, and jackets made of the skins of the less-sought-after lower animals . . . her locks had been so frequently and so drastically brightened and curled that to caress them, one felt, would be rather like running one's fingers through julienne potatoes."

"Her hair had the various hues of neglected brass."

And at the opposite end of the social spectrum from Mrs. Legion and her friends: "In general style and get-up the girls resemble a group of very clever female impersonators. They run to rather larger and more densely plumed hats that the fashion absolutely insists upon, and they don't go in for any of your dull depressing colours. Always heavily jeweled, they have an adroit way of mingling an occasional imitation bracelet or necklace with the genuine articles, happily confident that the public will be fooled. In the warm weather their dresses are of transparent material about the arms and shoulders, showing provocative glimpses of very pink ribbons and of lace that you could hardly tell from the real."

Pope had it that "the proper study of mankind is man." Dorothy Parker made hers a study of womankind that amounted to a dissection that no man would dare attempt if he valued his life. She was critical of so many affectations because

MRS. GORDON: How do you like my hair?

MRS. LAUTERBACH: Lovely. I can't wait for mine to go gray, so I can have it made blue.

(*The Ladies of the Corridor*)

"The lady at the employment agency was built in terraces. . . . She bit into each of her words and seemed to find it savoury, and she finished every sentence to the last crumb."

("Mrs. Hofstadter on Josephine Street")

"Mrs. Hazelton said: 'It's only I've always been told nothing ages a woman so much as being seen at the theater in the evening with just another woman.'"

("A Bolt behind the Blue")

"There is a persistent sweetness about Miss Oddie that will not be downed. . . . This determined saccharinity of Miss Oddie's is a phenomenon observable in many extremely unmarried women of—as the saying goes—a certain age; her unused affections have, as it were, turned to sugar; one might say that she has diabetes of the emotions."

("Our Tuesday Club")

she feared—as Mr. Benchley warned—that she suffered from many of them herself.

For all her criticism of New York society, she never ceased to be a part of it—for the simple reason that, whatever she found to be wrong with it, anywhere else was infinitely worse.

When her phone rang, she was in the habit of saying, "What fresh hell is this?" But she always picked up. The hell you probably knew was preferable to the alternative.

Her interest in it continued to her death. Who was sitting in her old place at "21"—Jack & Charlie's in the old speakeasy days? What were they talking about? Who was *writing* about today's Beautiful People?

"I love to read about them. . . . The women and the men that will write about them start out by being flippant. But they get so envious. They're like the little boy with his nose pressed against the bake shop window, you know, wanting to get in."

Once Dorothy Parker was "in," she never seriously tried to get out.

In the book *Living Authors*, published in 1932, when she was at the peak of her powers, was the following extract:

> At Mrs. Parker's apartment in the Algonquin Hotel a good portion of New York's smart literary set gathers daily at five. She is slightly over five feet in height, dark, and attractive, with somewhat weary eyes and a sad mouth. Her clothes come from Paris. Her favorite possession is Robinson, a dachshund. She is superstitious, pessimistic, and hates to be alone. Being extremely near-sighted, she wears glasses when writing, but has never been seen on the street with them. Flowers and a good cry are reported to be among her favorite diversions.

The New Yorker and Its "Constant Reader"

I hate Books;
They tire my eyes.

—"Books: A Hymn of Hate"

It is our national joy to mistake for the first rate, the
fecund rate.

—Reviewing Sinclair Lewis's *Dodsworth*

This is not a novel to be tossed aside lightly. It should
be thrown with great force.

—Reviewing a novel

I would liefer adopt the career of a blood donor.

—On being a book reviewer

Its general tenor will be of gaiety, wit and satire, but it will be more than a jester. It will not be what is commonly called radical or high brow. It will be what is commonly called sophisticated in that it will assume a reasonable degree of enlightenment on the part of its readers. It will hate bunk . . .

—*The New Yorker* mission statement

Humor, to my mind, is encapsulated in criticism. There must be a disciplined eye and a wild mind. There must be a magnificent disregard of your reader, for if he cannot follow you, there is nothing you can do about it.

—On being a reviewer

ON FEBRUARY 21, 1925, Harold Ross did what he had long been threatening to do. He brought out the first edition of his magazine, *The New Yorker*—a publication distinctly "not for the little old lady in Dubuque." Though why specifically "Dubuque" was never made entirely clear.

To begin with, the Algonks were little more than "advisory editors"—a title that Ross had given them without even asking their permission. A couple of years later, though, when it had become surprisingly successful, they had emigrated there en masse.

From its second issue, Dorothy Parker contributed verse and short stories as well as reviews. As with Crowninshield, she found her new boss a "lovely man," if a trifle eccentric.

"Ross like Heathcliffe, whom he in no other way resembled, went by just one name. There must, of course, have been those who called him Mr. Ross, though never to his back, and semi-occasionally some abraded contributor to the magazine would howl 'Harold!' at him. But in all other instances he was Ross. His improbabilities started with his looks. His long body seemed to be only basted together, his hair was quills upon the fretful porpentine, his teeth were Stone-henge, and his clothes looked as if they had been brought up by somebody else. Poker-faced he was not. Expressions, sometimes several at a time, would race across his countenance, and always, especially when he thought no one was looking, not the brow alone but the whole expanse would be corrugated by his worries, his worries over his bitch-mistress and his magazine. But what he did and what he caused to be done with *The New Yorker* left his mark and his memory upon his times.

"The dictionary says firmly that 'sophisticated' means 'adulterated' and Ross was probably the least adulterated human being that ever walked. Moreover, his ignorance was a very Empire State Building among ignorances: you had to admire it for its size. He was as void of knowledge of all matters cultural, scientific and sociological as a child in a parochial orphanage. Yet his ignorance was not, as it so often is in an adult, either exasperating or tiresome. There was an innocence to it—no airs, no pretenses; if he did not know a thing, he asked about it. Usually the answer delighted him, and always it astonished him. I think it was his perpetual astonishment that kept him from ever in his life being bored."

The Parker–Ross relationship was never an entirely easy one, considering their very different dispositions.

"He took me, once upon a time, to see Nazimova in *The Cherry Orchard*. At first he sat silent. Then he said, and over and over through the evening, in the all-but-voiceless voice of one who comes suddenly upon a trove of shining treasure, 'Say, this is quite a play—quite a play!' He had not seen it before. He had not heard of it.

"Once I used the word 'stigmata' in a piece. The proof came to me from Ross with no questions: only the exclamation 'no such word' in the margin. When friendship was restored, Ross conceded that maybe 'stigmata' had something to do with defective vision."

He also had the quaint idea that staff members should show up in the office on a reasonably regular basis. He once made the mistake of asking Parker why she hadn't come in to write her regular piece. "Someone was using the pencil." He didn't ask twice.

Remembering those days at a distance of some thirty years, she concluded, "Only God or James Thurber could have invented Ross." And only God could have invented Thurber.

Working with him on *The New Yorker* in later years, Parker found a certain affinity for his cockeyed view of the battle of the sexes, in both line and print.

"These are strange people that Mr. Thurber has turned loose upon us. They seem to fall into three classes—the playful, the defeated and the ferocious. All of them have the outer semblance of unbaked cookies; the women are of a dowdiness so over-whelming that it becomes tremendous style. Once a heckler complained that the Thurber women have no sex appeal. 'They have for my men,' he said."

By that time, Ross was long dead, and the magazine—she felt—had seen its best days.

"I don't read [it] much these days. It always seems to be the same old story about somebody's childhood in Pakistan."

In 1927, she began her famous series of book reviews under the byline "Constant Reader." In all, she was to write forty-six pieces.

Stylistically she picked up where her *Vanity Fair* theater reviews had left off in 1920. They were a series of personal con-versations with the reader for which the book she was reviewing provided a convenient—and not always relevant—peg.

"It is true that the book is occasionally overwritten, that cer-tain points are hammered too heavily. But, as I was saying to the landlord only this morning, you can't have everything."

There would be the little stream-of-consciousness asides, such as "There I go being tender about things again; it's no won-der men forget me" and "I am the one who believes, when things are calm and peaceful, that there is a chance of their staying so. That is the way I have gone about all my life. I really must make a note on my desk calendar to have my head examined one day next week. I am beginning to have more and more piercing doubts that my fontanel ever closed up properly."

There was Nan Britton's account of her affair with President Harding (and the resulting love child), which the Society for the Suppression of Vice—run by one John S. Sumner—wished to seize from the printers:

"I admit I drank down the whole book; but one swallow would make a Sumner. (That should have been better. I wish I had more time. Something might have been made of that.)"

There was the concern about style, both her own—"It seems to me that there are parts of it that don't come off; I feel, a little uncomfortably, that (X) has not yet found himself as a novelist. ["Do not come off" and "found himself" both in one sentence! Tie that for coining phrases, if you can.]"—and other people's—"One must hope that somewhere there is somebody who can tell him to watch his pen; because if he doesn't, one of these fine days he is going to simile himself to death."

Her lines of dismissal linger long after the book lies forgotten. Who can remember Lucius Beebe's *Shoot If You Must*? But her description of it is unforgettable—"This must be a gift book. That is to say, a book which you wouldn't take on any other terms" or a science tome that "was written without fear and without research."

In *The Coast of Illyria*, Charles Lamb wrote, "It's a filthy fashion, this rage for publishing one's degradations. Today a writer has a single collision with the normal world, and he makes a whole book of his personal damages."

Parker's judgment on literary trends was just as incisive. Take the short story. In the Parker scheme of things, there were six types that should be avoided like the plague. The opening line told you all you needed to know:

1. "'Ho, Félipe, my horse and pronto!' cried El Sol."
2. "Everybody in Our Village loved to go by Granny Wilkins' cottage."

3. "The train chugged off down the long stretch of track, leaving the little new school-mistress standing alone on the rickety boards that comprised the platform of Medicine Bend station."
4. "The country club was ahum, for the final match of the Fourth of July Golf Tournament was in full swing."
5. "'I dunno ez I ought to be settin' here, talkin', when there's vittles to git fer the men-folks.'"
6. "'For God's sake, don't do it, Kid!' whispered Annie the Wop, twining her slim arms round the Kid's bull-like neck."

"But with these half-dozen exceptions, I read all the other short stories that separated the Ivory Soap advertisements from the pages devoted to Campbell's Soups. I read about bored and pampered wives who were right on the verge of eloping with slender-fingered, quizzical-eyed artists, but did not. I read of young suburban couples, caught up in the fast set about them, driven to separation by their false, nervous life, and restored to each other by the opportune illness of their baby. I read tales proving that Polack servant-girls have their feelings, too. I read of young men who collected blue jade, and solved mysterious murders on the side. I read stories of transplanted Russians, of backstage life, of shop-girls' evening hours, of unwanted grandmothers, of heroic collies, of experiments in child-training, of golden-hearted cow-punchers with slow drawls, of the comicalities of adolescent love, of Cape Cod fisher-folk, of Creole belles and beaux, of Greenwich Village, of Michigan Boulevard, of the hard-drinking and easy-kissing younger generation, of baseball players, sideshow artists and professional mediums. I read, in short, more damn tripe than you ever saw in your life."

The tripe was by no means restricted to the short stories she read. A reviewer must, perforce, review whatever comes between hard covers.

There was Dr. Thew Wright's *Appendicitis* (illustrated), the good doctor's mission being to "bring an understanding of appendicitis to the laity. . . . And it really is terribly hard to keep from remarking, after studying the pictures, 'That was no laity; that's my wife.' It is hard, but I'll do it if it kills me."

There was Professor William Lyon Phelps's *Happiness* ("a very slim volume indeed"). "There is this to be said for a volume such as *Happiness*. It is second only to a rubber duck as the ideal bathtub companion. It may be held in the hand without causing muscular fatigue or nerve strain, it may be nearly balanced back of the faucets, and it may be read through before the water has cooled. And if it slips down the drain pipe, all right, it slips down the drain pipe."

The Art of Successful Bidding by George Reith "is, I have no moment's doubt, a fine textbook. But it is well over my head. I can't even jump for it."

Nor was she much more comfortable with Mlle. V. D. Gaudel's *The Ideal System for Acquiring a Practical Knowledge of French (Just the French One Wants to Know)*. "The future is veiled, perhaps

---

FRONT VIEW OF THE ABDOMINAL CAVITY

It is good, I admit; it has nice nuances, there is rhythm to the composition, and clever management is apparent in the shadows. But my feeling is that it is a bit sentimental, a little pretty-pretty, too obviously done with an eye towards popularity. It may well turn out to be another "Whistler's Mother" or a "Girl with Fan." My own choice is the impression of "Vertical Section of Peritoneum." It has strength, simplicity, delicacy, pity and irony. Perhaps, I grant you, my judgment is influenced by my sentiment for the subject. For who that has stood, bareheaded, and beheld the Peritoneum by moonlight can gaze unmoved upon its likeness?

mercifully, and so I cannot say that never, while I live, shall I have occasion to announce in French: 'It was to punish your foster-brother'; but I know which way I would bet. It may be that some day I shall be in such straits that I shall have to remark: 'The friend of my uncle who took the quill feather bought a round black rice-straw hat trimmed with two long ostrich feathers and a jet buckle.' Possibly circumstances will so weave themselves that it will be just the moment for me to put in: 'Mr. Fouchet would have received some eel.' It might occur that I must thunder: 'Obey, or I will not show you the beautiful gold chain.' But I will be damned if it is ever to be of any good to me to have at hand Mlle. Gaudel's masterpiece: 'I am afraid he will not arrive in time to accompany me on the harp.' "

At least *The Technique of the Love Affair* (by A Gentlewoman) rang a personal bell or two.

"If only it had been written and placed in my hands years ago, maybe I could have been successful, instead of just successive."

Occasionally, she would find a subject that genuinely engaged her sympathy and admiration, and when she did, the personal parallels were likely to shine through. One such was the late Katherine Mansfield, whose *Journals* she reviewed.

"She was not of the elite breed of the discontented; she was of the high few fated to be ever unsatisfied. Writing was the precious thing in life to her, but she was never truly pleased with anything she had written. With a sort of fierce austerity, she strove for the crystal clearness, the hard bright purity from which streams perfect truth. She never felt that she had attained them."

Another was dancer Isadora Duncan. In reviewing her autobiography, *My Life*, here was "a magnificent, generous, gallant, reckless, fated fool of a woman . . . a great woman . . . there was never a place for her in the ranks of the terrible, slow army of the cautious. She ran ahead, where there were no paths. . . . She was not a lucky lady." She might have been describing herself.

But anyone who liked a Katherine Mansfield was likely to loathe a Margot Asquith.

"That gifted entertainer, the Countess of Oxford and Asquith, author of *The Autobiography of Margot Asquith* (four volumes, neatly boxed, suitable for throwing purposes). . . . The affair between Margot Asquith and Margot Asquith will live as one of the prettiest love stories of all literature."

Milady pushed her luck by bringing out a second work and calling it *Lay Sermons*. Mrs. Parker found it to be "a book of essays with all the depth and glitter of a worn dime. A compilation of her sentiments, suitably engraved upon a nice, big calendar, would make an ideal Christmas gift for your pastor, your dentist, or Junior's music teacher. Through the pages walk the mighty. I don't say that Margot Asquith actually permits us to rub elbows with them ourselves, but she willingly shows us her own elbow, which has been, so to say, honed on the mighty."

The author expressed coy doubts about the suitability of the word "Sermons" to go with "Lay": "Happier, I think it would have been if, instead . . . she had selected the word 'Off.'"

Parker would claim that she usually turned to older writers "for comfort" and named *Vanity Fair* as her favorite novel. "I was a woman of eleven when I first read it," and she had since read it "about a dozen times a year."

Her beloved Dickens was another favorite—but most others had to fend for themselves.

CLASSICS

The Lives and Times of John Keats,
Percy Bysshe Shelley, and
George Gordon Noël, Lord Byron

Byron and Shelley and Keats
Were a trio of lyrical treats.
The forehead of Shelley was cluttered with curls,

And Keats never was a descendant of earls,
And Byron walked out with a number of girls,
But it didn't impair the poetical feats
Of Byron and Shelley,
Of Byron and Shelley.
Of Byron and Shelley and Keats.

Charles Dickens
Who call him spurious and shoddy
Shall do it o'er my lifeless body.
I heartily invite such birds
To come outside and say those words!

Walter Savage Landor
Upon the work of Walter Landor
I am unfit to write with candor.
If you can read it, well and good;
But as for me, I never could.

Alfred, Lord Tennyson
Should Heaven send me any son,
I hope he's not like Tennyson.
I'd rather have him play a fiddle
Than rise and bow and speak an idyll.

George Sand
What time the gifted lady took
Away from paper, pen, and book,
She spent in amorous dalliance
(They do those things so well in France)

("A Pig's Eye View of Literature")

In Paris, she would occasionally catch a glimpse of James
Joyce scurrying along. She found him taciturn in the extreme. "I
guess he's afraid he might drop a pearl."

O f the then-current crop of writers, the ladies perhaps had the most to fear from the Parker pen. Romantic novelist Elinor Glyn—the inventor of "It"—had a new offering. Her heroine was Ava, and Mrs. Parker introduces us to her.

"Ava was young and slender and proud. And she had it. It; hell; she had Those. . . . She was one who could not Give All unless she loved. Call it her hard luck, if you will, but that's how she was. . . . She could have made any All-American team in a moment, just on her dexterity at intercepting passes."

There was Kathleen Norris ("Who Believed in the Commercial Imperative").

"Remember, this is a book by Kathleen Norris . . . everything is going to turn out for the best, and there will never be a word that could possibly give pain to any of her readers and make sales fall off."

There was even controversial evangelist Aimée Semple McPherson, who dared risk *her* all with an autobiography.

"It may be that this autobiography is set down in sincerity, frankness, and simple effort. It may be, too, that the Statue of Liberty is situated in Lake Ontario.

"On the occasion that she drifts into longer and broader sentences, she writes as many other three-named authoresses have written before. Her manner takes on the thick bloom of rich red plush. The sun becomes 'that round orb of day' (as opposed, I expect, to those square orbs you see around so much lately). . . . It is difficult to say whether Mrs. McPherson is happier in her crackling exclamations or in her bead-curtain-and-chenille-fringe style. Presumably the lady is happy in both manners. That would make her two up on me."

Even a fellow Round Tabler like Edna Ferber ("surely America's most successful writeress. . . I'm told she whistles at her typewriter") had to learn to play the hand Dorothy Parker dealt. Years later, Parker said of her novel *Ice Palace*, "The book, which is going to be a movie, has the plot and characters of a book which is going to be a movie."

Nor did the menfolk fare any better. She felt that most of them were trading on hopelessly inflated reputations—reputations that were rapidly undermining whatever genuine talent they originally possessed.

In the late 1920s, Sinclair Lewis was generally considered to be America's preeminent "social" novelist—but not by Dorothy Parker. "Mr. Lewis is no longer the reporter; he has become the parodist." In fact, he became the synonym for the prolix in prose. Overhearing a group of gabby midwestern governors at a New York nightclub, she remarked, "Sounds like over-written Sinclair Lewis."

In reviewing his latest novel, *Dodsworth*, she summed up what, in her opinion, was wrong with current American literature. The most prolific writers were not necessarily the most professional.

"A list of our authors who have made themselves most beloved and, therefore, most comfortable financially, shows that it is our national joy to mistake for the first rate, the fecund rate."

Nor did the undeniable gravitas of Theodore Dreiser weigh too heavily on her.

"He is regarded, and I wish you could gainsay me, as one of our finest contemporary authors; it is the first job of a writer who demands rating among the great, or even among the good, to write well. If he fails that, as Mr. Dreiser, by any standard, so widely muffs it, he is, I think, unequipped to stand among the big. . . . To me Dreiser is a dull, pompous, dated and *darned near ridiculous writer*. All right. Go on and bring your lightning bolts."

> Theodore Dreiser
> Should ought to
> write nicer.

So who *did* she like? Ernest Hemingway. So much so that her enthusiasm almost tripped her up. Reviewing his collection *Men Without Women*, she wrote, "He is, to me, the greatest living writer of short stories." At which several people pointed out that Rudyard Kipling and Max Beerbohm were not without their supporters. Mrs. Parker felt the need to express her mea culpa in print.

"'Oh, my God,' I said—I was brought up in a mining town, and the old phrases come back in moments of emotion. . . . Maybe this would do better . . . 'Ernest Hemingway is, to me, the greatest American short story writer who lives in Paris most of the time but goes to Switzerland to ski, served with the Italian Army during the World war, has been a prize-fighter and has fought bulls, is coming to New York in the spring, is in his early thirties, has a black moustache, and is still waiting for that two hundred francs I lost to him at bridge.' Or maybe, after all, the only thing to do is to play safe and whisper: 'Ernest Hemingway is, to me, a good writer.'"

Asked, "Does he talk like he writes?" she responded, "Yes, he does talk like he writes. In fact, liker."

Hemingway—she would enthuse—"could sell a six day bicycle race to a Mother Superior. . . . All that remains to be said is that he is . . . the lost Dauphin, that he was shot as a German spy and that he is actually a woman masquerading in a man's clothes."

From the early 1930s, there were many writers who began to write in Hemingway's pared-down style, but they got short shrift from "Constant Reader." One of them was Dashiell Hammett, generally considered the originator of the "private eye" novel.

"He has all the mannerism of Hemingway, with no inch of Hemingway's scope nor flicker of Hemingway's beauty. . . . It is true that he is so hard-boiled you could roll him on the White House lawn. And it is also true that he is a good, hell-bent, cold-hearted writer, with a clear eye for the ways of hard women and a fine ear for the words of hard men. . . . Dashiell Hammett is as American as a sawed-off shotgun."

It was, perhaps, small wonder that Hammett—who was to become the life companion of her friend Lillian Hellman—disliked Parker to the point where, when she came to visit, he would move out.

She much preferred the work of her fellow Algonk and sometime lover Ring Lardner, whose premature death robbed American literature of what might have been a significant body of work.

"His unparalleled ear and eye, his strange, bitter pity, his utter sureness of characterization, his unceasing investigation, his beautiful economy . . . his qualities are not to be listed but to be felt, as you read his work."

Dorothy Parker, book reviewer and vivisectionist, put aside her *New Yorker* pen in 1931 and thought she had done so for good. But a quarter century later, her circumstances had changed decidedly for the worse, and she needed the money her old friend Arnold Gingrich, editor of *Esquire*, was offering her to be *his* "Constant Reader."

Gingrich was prepared to pay her $750 a week at a time when her political views had made her unemployable and her drinking problems professionally unreliable. She began work in 1957, and by 1958 Gingrich could reflect ruefully that "it is a high-forceps delivery every time we manage to get a piece out of her." The review copies would pile up, and many a week she would miss her deadline, using her imagination in inventing excuses that would have been properly employed in writing the review. Sometimes, she admitted, she didn't even *read* the book—just the cover blurb. Nonetheless, the Gingrich check arrived without fail.

And what did she find in this brave new literary world? In many ways, more of the same. There was still a plethora of "lady novelists": "As artists they're rot, but as providers they're oil wells; they gush." A good example—in the great tradition of the three name novelist—being Katherine Anne Porter and her *Ship of Fools*.

"To those of us who, after filling a postcard, are obliged to lie down and have wet cloths applied to our brows, this is not a book. It's the Pyramid."

But there was good news among the bad news.

"In all reverence I say Heaven bless the Whodunit, the soothing balm on the wound, the cooling hand on the brow, the opiate of the people."

As for the contemporary crop of writers, Dreiser was gone, but James Gould Cozzens was bidding fair to take his place with

PARKER   FAULKNER

the interminable *By Love Possessed* (1957), which "seemed to me cold, distant, and exasperatingly patronizing." Fortunately, there was still William Faulkner, "a vulnerable country boy" but "the man I believe to be the greatest writer we have."

Of the rest, she admired Saul Bellow and John O'Hara ("a genius") and thought that James Baldwin "can write like hell." She found Peter De Vries boring and Mary McCarthy "really trying." She was "uninterested" in John Updike but had a good word to say for his *The Poorhouse Fair*. "Perhaps this is a purely personal matter, but I am always drawn to reading a book about a poorhouse—after all, it is only normal curiosity to find out what it will be like in my future residence." But what still exercised her most was the apparent lack of attention paid to what a writer was put on earth to do, and the dismissive critical reception being accorded to the young Truman Capote brought it to a head.

"I am sick of those who skate fancily over the work of Mr. Capote. . . . They neglect to say one thing which is, to me, the most important; Truman Capote can *write*."

"I will say of the writers of today that some of them, thank God, have the sense to adapt to their times. Mailer's *The Naked and the Dead* is a great book. And I thought William Styron's *Lie Down in Darkness* an extraordinary thing. The start of it took your heart and flung it over there. . . . I love Sherlock Holmes. My life is so untidy and he's so neat. But as for the living novelists, I suppose E. M. Forster is the best, not knowing what that is, but at least he's a semi-finalist, wouldn't you think?"

One significant difference she found in the fiction of the 1950s and 1960s was the prevalence of outspoken sex, which she found both unnecessary and distasteful. It had been bad enough in the old days, when she had been prompted to write, "After this week's course of reading, I'm good and through with the whole matter of sex. I say it's spinach, and I say the hell with it!"

But now, "Certainly nobody wants to complain about sex itself, but I think we all have a legitimate grievance in the fact that, as it is shown in present day novels, its practitioners are so unmercifully articulate about it. . . . There is no more cruel destroyer of excitement than painstaking detail. Who reads these play-by-play reports of passion responds with much the same thrill as he would experience in looking over the blueprints for some stranger's garage. . . .

"The nowadays ruling that no word is unprintable has, I think, done nothing whatever for beautiful letters. The short flat terms used over and over, both in dialogue and narrative, add neither vigor nor clarity; the effect is not of shock, but of something far more dangerous—tedium.

"Obscenity is too valuable a commodity to chuck around all over the place; it should be taken out of the safe on special occasions only. . . . So I am growing old, a process that goes on at a gallop even as I sit here, for I find my heart turns tenderly to that yesterday when there were those two demure dashes between the first and fourth letters of the words used with telling frequency. . . . Can you remember, venerable subscriber, the days when there used to be rows of asterisks? How those little stars twinkled and gleamed, and how warmly they shone upon the imagination!

"I should like to issue a short, stiff statement, to be notarized if considered necessary, that I am through and done with novels containing scenes in which young ladies stand mothernaked before long mirrors, and evaluate, always favorably, their unveiled surfaces. Further, I will have no more of books in which various characters tell their dreams; tell, with prodigious extension of memory and ruthless courtesy to details, dreams which, unlike yours and mine, have to do with the plot of the piece. And finally and forever, I am come to the parting of the ways from works where Nature lore invades the telling of the tale. When the author gives me a scene of wild young passion, then I can no longer slog through the immediate follow-up of a tender description of the bendings of wheat in the breeze, nor yet of a report on the intricate delicacies of fern fronds, nor again of the fact that the wild jonquils are thicker than ever this year. . . . I realize that all this will cut down my reading drastically, nevertheless—There!"

CHAPTER

7

The Sexes

Oh, life is a glorious cycle of song,
A medley of extemporanea;
And love is a thing that can never go wrong,
And I am Marie of Roumania.

. . . Princes, never I'd give offense,
Won't you think of me tenderly?
Here's my strength and my weakness, gents—
I loved them until they loved me

—"Ballade at Thirty-Five"

The sun's gone dim, and
The moon's turned black;
For I loved him, and
He didn't love back.

—"Two Volume Novel"

71

Scratch a lover, and find a foe!
                          —"Ballade of a Great Weariness"

And if you do not like me so,
To hell, my love, with you.

                          —"Indian Summer"

I T WAS NOËL COWARD who defined love as "that age old devastating disease," but Dorothy Parker would have agreed with him—and then some. With her, it was never an illness; it was an epidemic.

In many ways, she was one of the first of the feminists. And yet—perhaps because of the times in which she lived and had her subversive being—she never glossed over the realities in the see-saw of the sexes, however unpalatable and personally inconvenient they might be.

"Men don't like nobility in women. Not any man. I suppose it is because men like to have the copyrights on nobility—if there is going to be anything like that in a relationship. . . .

"A man defending husbands versus wives, or men versus women, has got about as much chance as a traffic policeman trying to stop mad dogs by blowing two whistles."

"Most good women are hidden treasures who are only safe because nobody looks for them. . . .

Woman lives but in her Lord
Count to ten and man is bored.
                          "General Review of the Sex Situation"

"Woman's life must be wrapped up in a man."

"Women and elephants never forget."
                          "Ballade of Unfortunate Mammals"

"Wives are people who think that when the telephone rings it is against the law to answer it. . . .

"Wives are people whose watch is always a quarter-of-an-hour off . . . but they would have no idea what time it is, anyway, as daylight saving gets them all balled up. . . .

"Wives are people who get invited out somewhere and the husband asks if he ought to shave and they say, 'No, you look all right.' And when they get to wherever they are going, they ask everybody to 'Please forgive Luke as he didn't have time to shave.'"

A wife is also the woman who was foolish enough to tell Dorothy Parker proudly that she had kept her husband for seven years. "Don't worry, if you keep him long enough he'll come back in style."

Falling in love was easy. *Staying* in love was the hard part.

"She tried to remember what they used to talk about before they were married. . . . It seemed to her that they never had had much to say to each other. . . . She had always heard that true love was inarticulate. Then, besides, there had always been kissing and things, to take up your mind. But it had turned out that true marriage was apparently equally dumb. And you can't depend on kisses and all the rest of it to while away the evenings, after seven years."

"I'll be the way I was when he first met me. Then maybe he'll like me again. I was always sweet, at first. Oh, it's so easy to be sweet to people before you love them. . . . They don't like you to tell them they've made you cry. They don't like you to tell them you're unhappy because of them. If you do, they think you're possessive and exacting. And then they hate you. They hate you when you say anything you really think. You always have to keep playing little games. Oh, I thought we didn't have to; I thought this was so big I could say whatever I meant. I guess you can't, ever. I guess there isn't ever anything big enough for that."

Almost certainly the observation most associated with Dorothy Parker is the couplet "News Item":

Men seldom make passes
At girls who wear glasses.

Next to *Macbeth*'s "Lead on, MacDuff" (which should, of course, read, "Lay on, MacDuff"), it must be the most misquoted of popular quotations. Nine people out of ten will tell you that "men *never* make passes," and it used to drive Parker wild, not simply because they got it wrong but because it was the only line of hers they knew. ("It's a terrible thing to have made a serious attempt to write verse and then be remembered for two lines like those. I must, even by accident, have said other things worth repeating, if the lazy sons-of-bitches bothered to find out.") It was also an observation with a highly personal relevance. She herself wore glasses when she was working but was seen to remove them rapidly when others were around, especially if the "other" was male.

New Yorker writer E. B. White wrote that "a writer should take care to be memorable . . . I can't remember *Moby Dick* but I can remember "men seldom make passes at girls who wear glasses," which should place Mistress Parker ahead of Melville but probably doesn't."

Insult was finally added to injury during her stint in Hollywood when producer Samuel Goldwyn told her, "You're a great poet. 'Men never make a pass at girls wearing eyeglasses.' That's a great poem and you wrote it."

The eye with which she observed her own sex was beady and unclouded.

"Emmy Lineham had always been described as a cute little trick, and she was therefore obliged to be rosy and to twitter."

"No living eye, of human being or caged wild beast or dear, domestic animal, had beheld Mrs. Lanier when she was not being wistful. She was dedicated to wistfulness, as lesser artists to words and paint and marble. . . . It is safe to assume that Mrs. Lanier was wistful in her bathroom, and slumbered soft in wistfulness through the dark and secret night."

"Mrs. Ewing was a short woman who accepted the obligation borne by so many short women to make up in vivacity
what they lack in number of inches from the ground. She was a
creature of little pats and prods, little crinklings of the eyes
and wrinklings of the nose, little runs and ripples of speech and
movement, little spirals of laughter."

"Mrs. Bain cried a little in pauses in the conversation. She
had always cried easily and often. Yet, in spite of her years of
practice, she did not do it well. Her eyelids grew pink and sticky,
and her nose gave her no little trouble, necessitating almost constant sniffling. She sniffled loudly and conscientiously, and frequently removed her pince-nez to wipe her eyes with a crumpled
handkerchief, gray with damp."

"Mrs. Martindale's breasts were admirable, delicate
yet firm, pointing one to the right, one to the left, 'angry at
each other,' as the Russians have it. . . . She was tall, and her
body streamed like a sonnet. Her face was formed all of trian-
gles, as a cat's is. . . . Mrs. Martindale lingered in her fragrant
forties. Has not afternoon been adjudged the fairest time of
the day?"

Female affectation in all its forms affected Parker. It might,
in essence, be harmless, but she felt it undermined her sex,
which—God knew—needed all the help it could get. The casual

Like blossom on its stem is poised your head,
Wrapped closely round with fragrant bands.
As roses' passionate heart, your mouth is red;
Like lilies in the wind, your long white hands.
Brighter the glance of you than summer star;
But, lady fair, how awful thick you are!

("Sonnet—1")

dropping of French phrases particularly enraged her. She once heard a social acquaintance say *"Tant pis!"* and from that moment on she never refrained from asking, "How's old *tant pis* these days? Still full of it?"

Virtually all the Parker dispatches in the Battle of the Sexes are from the front line—the observations of a woman obsessed with life, love, and the pursuit of unhappiness. She had little to say about the pleasures of home, hearth, and the pitter-patter of tiny feet. And what she did say was not exactly comforting.

"The best way to keep children home is to make the home atmosphere pleasant—and let the air out of the tires."

"I require only three things of a man. He must be handsome, ruthless and stupid." In that, Dorothy Parker defined both the requirements and the problem that would haunt her emotional life. Even allowing for the fact that—like so many of her statements—it was said to be remembered, it provides a field day for the psychologist. Here was a woman asking for superficiality and trouble from someone who would never challenge her intellectually. She was to find it repeatedly with "my little, easy loves."

In today's popular parlance, the psychologist would undoubtedly go on to say that the lady suffered from "low self-esteem" and cite her verse in particular as symptomatic:

> Here's my strength and weakness, gents—
> I loved them until they loved me.
> . . .
> For I loved him, and
> He didn't love me.
> . . .
> Some men break your heart in two,
> Some men fawn and flatter,
> Some men never look at you;
> And that cleans up the matter.
>
> ("Experience")

Oh, is it, then, Utopian
To hope that I may meet a man
Who'll not relate, in accents suave,
The tales of girls he used to have?

("De Profundis")

Never a suggestion that the course of true love would not contain some natural disaster—or, indeed, that there was any such thing:

And love is a thing that can never go wrong.
And I am Marie of Roumania.

In one of her stories, the heroine defines her "Vanished Dream" man—in a paraphrase of Parker's own words—as "an English-tailored Greek God, just masterful enough to be entertaining, just wicked enough to be exciting, just clever enough to be a good audience."

Her own Greek god, when he came along, was a Connecticut boy—Edwin Pond Parker II, age twenty-three, a stockbroker.

"He was beautiful but not very smart. He was supposed to be in Wall Street but that didn't mean anything."

He was "a handsome Gentile" and he had "a nice clean name." She married him in June 1917 to acquire that name. "That was all there was to it."

Well, perhaps not quite all. She seemed to enjoy the novelty of being a bride, but the war cut that short.

"We were married for about five minutes, then he went off to war. He didn't want to kill anybody, so he drove an ambulance. Unfortunately, they had dope in the ambulance. Morphine. You know, that's not good for you. Well, [after the war] it was one sanitorium after another."

And if it wasn't entirely true, it made a good story for lunch at the Algonquin. Eddie became the regular butt of the Parker jokes. "Did I tell you what Eddie did today?" When, a confirmed alcoholic, he finally returned from the front, he would hang around the Round Table with nothing much to contribute, except to light his wife's cigarettes and listen to her latest exaggeration and laugh on cue. She was the court jester and he the court jest.

Unable to hold a job, he soon returned to the family home in Connecticut, and it was there that Mrs. Parker eventually divorced him, in a state "where you can get it for roller skating." But that was not until March 31, 1928, and even then she hung on to her favorite possession from the marriage—her name.

In the meantime, there were lovers aplenty. But sadly,

> Every love's the love before
> In a duller dress.
> That's the measure of my love—
> Here's my bitterness:
> Would I knew a little more,
> Or very much less.
>
> ("Summary")

> They hail you as their morning star
> Because you are the way you are.
> If you return the sentiment,
> They'll try to make you different.
>
> ("Men")

> Oh, gallant was the first love, and glittering and fine;
> The second love was water, in a clear white cup;
> The third love was his, and the fourth was mine;
> And after that, I always get them all mixed up.
>
> ("Pictures in the Smoke")

> Though she's a fool who seeks to capture
> The twenty-first fine, careless rapture.
>
> ("A Fairly Sad Fale")

"Lips that taste of tears, they say, are the best for kissing,"

Charles MacArthur.

and young playwright Charles MacArthur certainly caused her plenty of tears in their brief and very public affair. Never again would Dorothy Parker willingly allow the Algonks to see her with her heart on her sleeve ("like a wet red stain").

MacArthur didn't just make her unhappy; he made her pregnant for the first time. ("It's not the tragedies that kill us. It's the messes. I can't stand messes.") Since they were both already married, there was no question of marriage, so Dorothy Parker experienced her first abortion. ("Serves me right for putting all my eggs in one bastard.") MacArthur contributed just thirty dollars to the cost of it ("like Judas making a refund").

After that she would act tougher, though she would never be any less vulnerable. She continued to walk around "with my head flung up" and carrying "between my ribs . . . a gleaming pain."

There was John Garrett, a "very good-looking young man indeed . . . a graceful young man ever carefully dropping references to his long, unfinished list of easy conquests." Garrett was typical of a whole subspecies of young men who were now drawn in shoals to the celebrity and wit of Dorothy Parker—who happened at that time to be extremely beautiful, too.

John McClain took things one stage further—as well as taking everything he could from Mrs. Parker. He didn't merely *talk* about his other women—he actively pursued them.

At a weekend party, Dorothy's friends were shocked to hear

I am not sick, I am not well.
My quondam dreams are shot to hell.
My soul is crushed, my spirit sore;
I do not like me any more.
I cavil, quarrel, grumble, grouse.
I ponder on the narrow house.
I shudder at the thought of men . . .
I'm due to fall in love again.

("Symptom Recital")

Harpo Marx (*standing*), Charles MacArthur, Dorothy, and Alexander Woollcott.

McClain on the phone making a date in front of her with a well-known society lady. When he had left, she turned to them with a shrug: "I have no squash courts. What can I do?" On a similar occasion, when he had gone off to join another socialite for a weekend, "He'll be back as soon as he has licked all the gilt off her ass."

But the most embarrassing public moment was when McClain picked a drunken fight with her in the lobby of the Algonquin—where she happened to be living at the time—in front of Benchley and Adams.

"And what's more, you're a lousy lay!" he shouted at her before he stormed off. In the ensuing silence, she said, "I'm afraid his body went to his head."

On one occasion during her prolonged—and largely unpaid-for—stay in the hotel, manager Frank Case is supposed to have knocked on her door and enquired, "Do you have a gentleman in your room?" "Just a minute—I'll ask him."

" 'A lover who pursues'—oh, think what that sounds like to one whose eyes have so often rested on the ugliest modern gesture: that of a man looking at his wristwatch!"

"I have sought, by study, to better my form and make myself Society's Darling. You see, I had been fed, in my youth, a lot of old wives' tales about the way men would instantly forsake a beautiful woman to flock around a brilliant one. It is but fair to say that, after getting out in the world, I had never seen this happen, but I thought that maybe I might be the girl to start the vogue. I would become brilliant. I would sparkle. I would hold whole dinner tables spellbound. I would have throngs fighting to come within hearing distance of me while the weakest, elbowed mercilessly to the outskirts, would cry, 'What did she say?' or 'Oh, please ask her to tell it again.' That's what I would do."

And, in large measure, that's what she did do. But the brilliant little lady they were all looking at in the heady 1920s and 1930s was also looking out from beneath her trademark bangs for one more handsome, ruthless, stupid male face:

Into love and out again.
Thus I went and thus I go.

" 'I'm sorry, darling.' . . . He smiled at her. She felt her heart go liquid, but she did her best to be harder won."

"He gave her a look you could have poured on a waffle. . . .

"He was a very good-looking young man indeed, shaped to

be annoyed. His voice was intimate as the rustle of sheets, and he kissed easily. There was no tallying the gifts of Charvet handkerchieves, *art moderne* ashtrays, monogrammed dressing-gowns, gold key-chains of thin wood, inlaid with views of Paris comfort stations, that were sent to him by ladies too quickly confident, and were paid for with the money of unwitting husbands, which is acceptable any place in the world."

The affairs became more and more perfunctory. She began to treat men as—she firmly believed—men routinely treated women. "I am cheap—you know that," she told Edmund Wilson.

There was the alcoholic interlude in 1929 with Laddie Sandford, the heir to a carpeting fortune: "We wouldn't even know each other, even if we ever did see each other again. And I don't even feel embarrassed about it, because I can't tell you how little sex means to me now . . . and polo players wouldn't count, anyway."

In later years, there was play collaborator Ross Evans, who had "the hue of availability." On another drink-induced occasion, she made love to him on a sofa with friends present. The next day, she apologized perfunctorily: "We must have been awfully picturesque."

"When the affair was over, she put sex carefully away on the highest cupboard shelf, in a box marked 'Winter Hats—1916.'"

> Authors and actors and artists and such
> Never know nothing, and never know much.
> Sculptors and singers and those of their kidney
> Tell their affairs from Seattle to Sydney.
> Playwrights and poets and such horse's necks
> Start off from anywhere, end up at sex.
> Diarists, critics and similar roe
> Never say nothing and never say no.
> People Who Do Things exceed my endurance;
> God, for a man that solicits insurance!

Had she ever met one, he would have told her she was a bad risk.

As Mrs. Parker got older, the men grew younger. In "Dusk before Fireworks," she comments on aging:

"'She says she has something she wants to tell me.'

'It can't be her age,' she said.

He smiled without joy. 'She says it's too hard to say over the wire,' he said.

'Then it may be her age,' she said. 'She's afraid it may sound like her telephone number.'"

One of her more disturbing stories, to my mind, is "Advice to the Little Peyton Girl" with its autobiographical and hopeless good advice.

"'You see, Sylvie,' Miss Marion said, 'men dislike dismal prophecies. I know Bunny Barclay is only twenty, but all men are the same age. And they all hate the same things. . . . Men hate straightening out unpleasantness. They detest talking things over. Let the past die, my child, and go easily on from its unmarked grave. . . . Love is like quicksilver in the hand. . . . Leave the fingers open and it stays in the palm. Clutch it, and it darts away.'"

As soon as Sylvie Peyton has left, Miss Marion is on the phone, harassing the (presumably married) man who refuses to take her calls.

In Dorothy Parker's observation of life's threadbare pageant, with age came indignity. On one occasion, she read aloud an extract from a book to Lillian Hellman in which a determined woman was pursuing a man who had said he didn't want to see her again. "That night she tried to climb in through the transom of his hotel room and got stuck at the hips." Closing the book, she

Should they whisper false of you
Never trouble to deny;
Should the things they say be true,
Weep and storm and swear they lie.

("Superfluous Advice")

turned to look at Hellman and said with straight face, "I've never got stuck at the hips, Lilly, and I want you to remember that."

"God, aren't all words connected with marriage horrible? Connubial, nuptial, spouse" (Paul in *The Ladies of the Corridor*).

In 1934, Mrs. Parker became Mrs. Alan Campbell—without ever ceasing to be "Mrs. Parker." Campbell was, naturally, handsome though not particularly stupid. He was also twenty-nine to Dorothy's forty. She declared herself to be "in a sort of coma of happiness." Life with Alan was "fun, a bundle of fun . . . lovelier than I ever knew anything could be."

"I love being a juvenile's bride and living in a bungalow—which she christened "Repent-at-Leisure"—"and pinching dead leaves off the rose bushes. I will be God damned!"

Even so, there was a worrying imbalance from the outset. "We have been down here without any servants," she wrote to Woollcott, "and life is housework and no other thing. Alan cooks and I clean, and who is then the gentleman? It isn't so much that I mind bed-making and sweeping and dish-washing as that I am undone by my incompetence. It takes me every minute of every day, and the results are such as would cause me to be fired without reference anywhere. This contributes generously to a low, brooding inferiority nagged along by the silent question, 'Well, for Christ's sake, what *are* you good for, anyway?'"

Nonetheless, age was becoming more and more of a factor, and she referred to it constantly: "I'm thinking of sending him to military school when he's old enough."

Nor was it long before the bloom was off the rose bushes. At first, the kidding was fairly kind—as it had been with Mr. Parker—and Campbell took it in good part when Dorothy referred to his early acting career. Alan, she would say, had been "one of those people who come in during the second act of a play, carrying a tennis racket with rhinestone strings, and ask the assembled company—'Who's for tennis?' . . . It was like watching a perfor-

Alan Campbell and Parker.

mance that Vassar girls would do, only *nicer* . . . all dressed as men, and you'd expect their hair to fall down any minute."

Two things prolonged the shelf life of their marriage. Alan was also ambitious to be a writer, and he persuaded Hollywood studios to hire them as a team on the strength of the Parker name—and they decided to play at building a real home and start a family.

In fact, there was a third thing. Alan Campbell genuinely loved Dorothy Parker.

The surrealistic experience of Hollywood—far more fictional than New York—determined her of one thing. "We've just got to have roots," she told Alan. All she wanted to do was "get out of the city, live in the country in a little white cottage with green shutters and fill my life with flowers, puppies and babies." A number of their friends had bought country homes in Bucks County, Pennsylvania, so that's where the Campbells went, too. But they never did find the "little white cottage with green shutters." Instead they bought a farm, Fox House, in over a hundred acres of land—which they proceeded to modernize in somewhat questionable taste.

"We caused talk. We even caused hard feelings. . . . There are no folk so jealous of countryside tradition as those who never before have lived below the twelfth floor of a New York building. They moved into their beautiful Pennsylvania stone house, and they kept their magazines in antique cradles, and they rested their cocktail glasses on cobblers' benches. . . . Their walls were hung with representations of hydrocephalic little girls with scalloped pantalets and idiotic lambs, and their floors were spread with carpets that some farmer's wife, fifty years ago, must have hated the sight of, and saved her egg money to replace. Now, they can't *really* think such things are a delight to live with. Can they? They found us vandals. . . . Now only the natives speak to us. We feel all right." She referred to her *New Yorker* critics as "Fifty-second Street Thoreaus."

Dorothy, to her joy, became pregnant, but—perhaps because of the abortions or because bearing a first child at the age of forty-three was predictably a chancy business—she lost the baby, at which point the fun went out of the whole project. Domesticity was clearly not in her destiny.

The gardening that had been such fun became a chore: "I'm awfully lazy about it—and the weeds are so much quicker than I am." And then there were those goddam *seasons* to contend with, particularly spring.

As early as 1928 a review had her complaining, "Oh, I feel terrible. Rotten, I feel. I've got Spring Misery. I've got a mean attack of Crocus Urge. I bet you I'm running a temperature right at this moment—running it ragged.

"I'm always this way in the Spring. Sunk in Springtime: or Take Away Those Violets. I hate the filthy season. Summer makes me drowsy. Autumn makes me sing. Winter's pretty lousy, but I hate Spring. They know what Spring makes out of me. Just a Thing That Was Once a Woman, that's all I am in the Springtime. But do they do anything about it? Oh, no. Not they. Every year back Spring comes, with the nasty little birds yapping their fool heads off, and the ground all mucked up with arbutus. Year after year after year."

When asked by an interviewer to describe her home in two words, she replied, "Want it?"

The relationship with Alan deteriorated rapidly. She accused him of being homosexual—"Have you met my friend, the wickedest woman in Paris?" In reality, he was probably bisexual.

"What am I doing in Hollywood at my age and married to a fairy? (It's the curved lips of those boys that's got him so interested)."

She was increasingly rude to him in public, much to the embarrassment of their friends: "I don't know why he should get so angry just because I called him a fawn's ass."

On one occasion, she had to absent herself from guests to finish a film script. "Do forgive me, but I have to go to that fucking thing upstairs," she said, referring to the script. Then, unable to resist adding the topper, "and I don't mean Alan Campbell."

Why is it no one ever sent me yet
One perfect limousine, do you suppose?
Ah, no, it's always just my luck to get
One perfect rose.

("One Perfect Rose")

Occasionally, one of her friends, who should have known better, would remonstrate with her: "You're married to a charming man who loves you. What more do you want?" "Presents," she replied petulantly.

In World War II, history repeated itself. Although overage for the draft by this time, in September 1942, Private Alan Campbell enlisted and was sent abroad, just as Edwin Parker had been before him.

Dorothy accompanied him to his enlistment in Philadelphia and was greatly moved by what she saw. She wrote to Woollcott, "Most of [the men] look poor—I mean by that, they haven't got coats on, they have soiled shirts and stained pants, their working clothes. The Lord God knows, those men who have made up their minds don't look poor in any other way and aren't poor! The majority of them are very young—'heart-breakingly young,' I read in a piece by a lady who watched the troops go by and threw them roses, which were their immediate need. They are not in the least heart-breaking, and I think if you were to call them that, they would turn out to be neck-breaking. They are young, certainly—several even had women standing beside them in line, their mommas, come to give consent to a minor's enlistment—but they're all right. . . . There were numerous Negroes. And nobody avoided them, as they stood in line with the whites, nobody shied away from them or stood in silence. They all talked with one another. . . . They all have their bags, and the only time I busted was at the sight of a tall, thin young

Negro . . . carrying a six-inch square of muslin in which were his personal effects. . . . And then I realized I was rotten to be tear-sprinkled. He wasn't sad. He felt fine. . . . I was ashamed of myself. And yet, dear Alec, I defy you to have looked at that and kept an arid eye. That, of course, has nothing to do with war. Except, of course, that a man who had no more than that was going to fight for it."

The induction ceremony gave rise to another less inspiring incident that was to haunt her ever after.

"So, while we were standing there, there came up to me a fat, ill-favored, dark little woman, who said to me—'Parn me, but aren't you Dorothy Parker? Well, I've no doubt you've heard of me, I'm Mrs. Sig Greesbaum, Edith Greesbaum, you'd probably know me better as. I'm the head of our local chapter of the Better Living Club, and we'd like to have you come talk to us. Of course, I'm still a little angry at you for writing that thing about men not making advances at girls who wear glasses, because I've worn glasses for years, and Sig, that's my husband, but I still call him my sweet-heart, he says it doesn't matter a bit, well, he wears glasses him-self. And I want you to talk to our club, of course, we can't pay you any money, but it will do you a lot of good, we've had all sorts of wonderful people, Ethel Grimsby Loe that writes all the greetings cards, and the editor of the *Doylestown Intelligencer*, and Mrs. Mercer, that told us all about Italy when she used to live there after the last war, and the photographs she showed us of her cypresses and all, and it would really be a wonderful thing for you to meet us, and now when can I put you down to come talk to us?'

"So I said I was terribly sorry, but if she didn't mind, I was busy at the moment. So she looked around at the rows of men— she hadn't seen them before, apparently; all they did was take up half the station—and she giggled heartily and said, 'Oh, what are those? More poor suckers caught in the draft?'

"And an almighty wrath came upon me, and I said, 'Those are American patriots who have volunteered to fight for your lib-erty, you sheeny bitch!' And I walked away, already horrified—as I am now—at what I had said. Not at the gist, which I will stick to and should, but the use of the word 'sheeny,' which, I give you my word, I have not heard for forty years and have never used before. The horror lies in the ease with which it came to me. And worse horror lies in the knowledge that, if she had been black, I would have said, 'You nigger bitch!' Dear God. The things I have fought against all my life. And that's what I did."

This time a more worldly war wife could offer advice to others. In 1944, she wrote a piece for *Vogue* called "Who Is That Man?"

"You say goodnight to your friends, and know that tomorrow you will meet them again, sound and safe as you will be. It is not like that where your husband is. There are the comrades, closer in friendship to him than you can ever be, whom he has seen comic or wild or thoughtful; and then broken or dead. There are some who have gone out with a wave of the hand and a gay obscenity, and have never come back. We do not know such things; prefer, and wisely, to close our minds against them. . . .

"I have been trying to say that women have the easier part in war. But when the war is over—then we must take up. The truth is that women's work begins when the war ends, begins on the day their men come home to them. For who is that man who will come back to you? You know him as he was; you have only to close your eyes to see him sharp and clear. You can hear his voice whenever there is silence. But what will he be, this stranger that comes back? How are you to throw a bridge across the gap that has separated you—and that is not the little gap of months and miles? He has seen the world aflame; he comes back to your new red dress. He has known glory and horror and filth and dignity; he will listen to you tell of the success of the canteen dance, the upholsterer who disappointed, the arthritis of your aunt. What have you to offer this man? . . . There have been people you never knew with whom he has had jokes you would not comprehend and talks that would be foreign to your ear. There are pictures hanging in his memory that he can never show to you. Of this great part of his life, you have no share . . . things forever out of your reach, far too many and too big for jealousy. That is where you start and from there you go on to make a friend out of that stranger from across a world."

The advice was sound, but she could not follow it herself.

On May 27, 1947, she divorced Campbell. Fox House had been sold two years earlier for a loss of $80,000. There were to be no more cottages with roses around the door. Countless puppies, yes, but no babies. All of that was over.

But, as it turned out, not *quite* over. The Campbells were a couple who couldn't live with each other, but they couldn't live without each other, either. In 1950, the couple remarried, slightly to their own surprise. "Who in life," Dorothy asked rhetorically, "gets a second chance?" Recounting the wedding day: "People who haven't talked to each other in years are on speaking terms again today—including the bride and groom."

To say that it was a happy ending would be to stretch the truth into fiction. For as long as it lasted, it was an armed truce, a mutual dependence they both needed as their lives—both jointly and separately—began to unravel.

On June 14, 1963, Dorothy woke to find Alan in bed beside her, dead of a drug overdose taken while he was drunk. Even though the coroner gave it the benefit of a verdict of accidental death, it was generally supposed to have been suicide. He was fifty-nine and Dorothy seventy-one.

At the funeral, a neighbor, Mrs. Jones, asked the widow if there was anything she could do for her. "Get me a new husband." Appalled, Mrs. Jones replied, "I think that is the most callous and disgusting remark I ever heard in my life."

"So sorry. Then run down to the corner and get me ham and cheese on rye and tell them to hold the mayo."

"Woman's life must be wrapped up in a man, and the cleverest woman on earth is the biggest fool with a man."

"The fucking you get isn't worth the fucking you get."

Dogs: A Digression

I always call dogs "he." It don't do to notice everything.
> —Mrs. Gordon in *The Ladies of the Corridor*

Don't let me take any horses home with me. It doesn't matter so much about stray dogs and kittens, but elevator boys are awfully stuffy when you try to bring in a horse. . . . You can always tell that the crash is coming when I start getting tender about Our Dumb Friends. Three highballs, and I think I'm St. Francis of Assisi.
> —"Just A Little One"

Sic—*as in dog.*
> —Dorothy Parker

Bonne Bouche was all that Mrs. Hazleton could ask of a pet. She was tiny, she was noiseless, and she had a real talent for sleeping.

—"The Bolt Behind the Blue"

LTHOUGH SHE invariably found people disappointing, Dorothy Parker found a sort of solace in her dogs ("Four-legged people—but nicer"). In her mature years, she was rarely seen without them, nestled on her lap or tucked away under her bar stool into the small hours.

It all started as a by-product of her dysfunctional family life at the turn of the century, when, as a young child largely ignored by her siblings, she poured out her affection on the pack of undomesticated French bulldogs and Boston terriers—Rags, Nogi, and Bunk—who were allowed the run of the Rothschild house. They would be reincarnated many times over—as would their erratic household habits.

In no particular order there was Amy—the stray she picked up in the street when she saw a truck driver trying to kick it. Instead, Mrs. Parker kicked the truck driver, snatched up the dog, and took it to the nearby studio of her friend, painter Neysa McMein, where it proceeded to eat all the rose madder paint.

A Scottie that Alexander Woollcott christened "AWP" when the dog managed to "christen" Woollcott three times in a single car ride.

A poodle called Cliché "because the streets are carpeted with black French poodles."

A blue Bedlington terrier called John: "I picked him out because Bedlingtons are trained to root up gardens and hunt otters, and my New York apartment was simply infested with otters." John contracted mange. ("He *said* he got it from a lamp post.")

When she lived with Eddie Parker, they had a Boston terrier she called Woodrow Wilson "because he was full of shit." Her failure to housebreak him did nothing for the condition of the apartment. ("Yes, it does seem a bit Hogarthian.") Nor was

Dorothy Parker with her dachshund, Robinson (1962).

the decor helped by the presence of a canary named Onan "because he spilled his seed upon the ground."

Her regular New York haunts learned to tolerate the Parker pet foibles, but Hollywood was a different story. When her current dog behaved in the lobby of the Beverly Hills Hotel as it was used to behaving at home, the manager was understandably irate.

"Miss Parker, look what your dog just did!"

Drawing herself up to her full five feet and nothing much, she replied haughtily, "*I* did it," and walked on. But after that, she left the dogs at home and referred to the hotel ever after as "the place where the elephants go to die."

It was, after all, not an isolated incident. When her dog was sick on the carpet in the middle of a party, she was heard to mutter, "It's the company."

Her experience taught her only one invaluable lesson: "I do believe that you should select for your personal use, if you live in the city, a dog whose size recommends himself for metropolitan life. Anything larger than a Shetland pony is perhaps a shade impractical. . . . There was that Airedale I had once, I remember. It was during his reign that my apartment came to be known as the Black Hole of Calcutta.

"You see, when he came into my life, he was seven weeks old and about the size of a three-dollar Teddy bear. And an Airedale would appear to be an entirely suitable dog for city-wear; you see thousands of them . . . walking carefree and unconcerned along the avenues, usually with very pretty ladies respectfully occupying the other end of their leashes. But this was a sort of super-Airedale. In the wholesome air and sunlight of Manhattan, he grew and he grew until many people advised my entering him in the horse show. We would go out for a little walk, he and I, and my feet would never be on the ground during the entire excursion.

"Indoors he developed the habit of sofa-eating; he became indeed, a veritable addict. Give that dog an ordinary sofa, such as your furniture dealer would be glad to let you have for a nominal sum, and he could make a whole meal off it. If you ran out of sofas, he would be philosophical about the matter—he was always delightfully good—and make a light snack of a chintz-covered arm chair. Once, I recall, he went a-gypsing and used a set of Dickens, the one with the Cruikshank illustrations, for a picnic lunch."

Eventually, she gave the dog to some friends who lived in the country.

"There was a sad scene at our parting. I was the sad scene. He never gave me so much as a backward look. But that is ever my story. My dearest wish would be to be one to whom dogs gave all their devotion; but they always cast me off like a withered violet when anyone else comes in the room. It is their indifference, I suppose, that holds me."

In "Love Fashion, Love Her Dog," she advised the readers of *Vogue* on how to view a dog as a fashion accessory.

"When a woman has a wardrobe stocked with bulldogs, and the style suddenly changes to Scottish terriers, what is she going to do about it? She can't have them made over, unfortunately. She might lay them aside, for the proverbial seven years, until they become fashionable again. She might even bestow them, with her antiquated clothes, on some deservedly poor family. She might send them to the country to rest their jangled nerves after their social season."

One of the few advantages she found in Hollywood was that there she and her dogs had room to breathe.

"I love a big yard full of dogs. There are two additions—a four-months-old dachshund, pure enchantment, named Fraulein, and a mixed party called Scrambles who is, by a happy coincidence, the one dog in the world you couldn't love. This gap in her character causes us to lean over backwards to ply her with attentions, and so she's worse than ever. You don't know anybody who wants a half-Welsh terrier, half-Zambi, do you?"

Dogs—even at secondhand—helped her through her Hollywood hell. A telegram to a friend read, "IN ORDER TO WISH YOU A HAPPY CHRISTMAS I AM INTERRUPTING WORK ON MY SCREEN EPIC—LASSIE GET DOWN."

One film she was involved with featured a canine performer. "They got one who looked little short of ideal but he wasn't really bright. They just plain couldn't make him do anything he was supposed to do, so finally in their despair, they put him on wires. Day upon day, they jerked him through his scenes like a marionette, which was, understandably, wearing, and the director was beside himself. After they had gone through one scene with him more than sixty times, the embittered man threw down his megaphone and cried, 'This can't go on! We'll have to

Your manners are a total loss,
Your morals, something awful.
Perhaps you'll ask, as many do,
What I endure your thrall for?
'Twas ever thus—it's such as you
That women always fall for.

("To My Dog")

put another wire on him.' And the cameraman, who was peering through his frame, said, 'Christ, he looks like a zither now.'"

In France she bought a Scottie called (by a previous owner) Daisy. Daisy was smart but oblivious to the wishes of her new owner. "Why, that dog is practically a Phi Beta Kappa. She can sit up and beg, and she can give her paw—I don't say she *will*, but she can."

On another occasion in Munich, it was a thoroughbred dachshund, Eiko von Blutenberg, she promptly renamed Robinson. "He has no sense and so is at ease in any drawing room." Back in New York, Robinson was her constant companion, so much so that when she finally retired for what was left of the night, she would give the dog one of her sleeping pills so that he did not wake too early in the morning.

Poor Robinson came to a sad end. He was attacked by a much larger dog and badly mauled. When the owner of the other dog tried to claim that Robinson had started it, Mrs. Parker replied witheringly, "I have no doubt he was also carrying a revolver." Sadly, Robinson did not survive the incident, throwing her into a deep depression.

Other animals did occasionally cross the Parker path. Climbing into a taxi one day, she found herself sharing it

"Whatever is, is good," your gracious creed.
You wear your joy of living like a crown.
Love lights your simplest act, your every deed.
(Drop it, I tell you—put that kitten down!)
You are God's kindliest gift of all,—a friend.
Your shining loyalty unflecked by doubt,
You ask but leave to follow to the end.
(Couldn't you wait until I took you out?)

("Verse for a Certain Dog")

with two baby alligators the previous passenger had thought-
fully forgotten. Hurrying home, she put them in the bathtub
and went about her business. She returned to find a note from
her maid: "I will not be back. I cannot work in a house where
there are alligators. I would have told you this before, but I didn't
suppose the question would ever come up."

Leaving a hostelry on Sixth Avenue, she saw a cab horse and
decided he looked tired and in need of a friend, so she went over
and kissed him. She said she'd be happy to kiss him again and
even go to Atlantic City with him if he were to ask her. "I don't
care what they say about me. Only I shouldn't like to have that
horse going around thinking he has to marry me."

Or there was the time Woollcott was agonizing about
putting down an unwanted litter of kittens. How *did* one kill a
cat? "Have you tried curiosity?" (or, in another version of the
same story, "kindness").

In Hollywood, she and Woollcott were invited to dinner by
a host who lived near the edge of a wood and was in the habit of
putting out food to draw out the wild animals for the delight
and amusement of his guests. On the first night, nothing happened. The host insisted they return the following night. Still
no show. "Well," said the perpetually helpful Mrs. Parker, "I
thought we'd at *least* get the after-theatre crowd."

"Animals are much better than people. God, I love animals. . . . Look, I'll tell you what let's do, after we've had just
a little highball. Let's go out and pick up a lot of stray dogs. I
never had enough dogs in my life, did you? We ought to have
more dogs."

At the very end of her life, her dogs were Dorothy Parker's
only companions. Troisième (Troy), Misty, and finally the dog
her closest friend, Beatrice Ames Stewart, rushed round to res-
cue from the apartment when she heard of Dorothy's death. She
knew that the last thing Mrs. Parker would have wished was for
her pal to end up in the pound.

The dog's name was C'est Tout.

CHAPTER

9

Writer at Work

Remember what I tell you when you're choosing
a career:
"Take in laundry work; cart off dust;
Drive a moving van if you must;
Shovel off the pavement when the snow lies white;
But think of your family, and please don't write."

—"Grandfather Said It"

Dear God, please make me stop writing like a woman.
For Jesus Christ's sake, Amen.

—Dorothy Parker

I haven't got a visual mind. I hear things.

—Dorothy Parker

ZABEL: *Precision is the basis of style.*

—*The Ice Age*

I want so much to write well, though I know I don't,
and that I didn't make it. But during and at the end
of my life, I will adore those who have.

—Dorothy Parker

D OROTHY PARKER was as ambivalent about her writing as she was about her men. If she had done it, it couldn't—despite all the acclaim—be any good.

"The trick about her writing is the trick about Ernest Hemingway's writing," wrote Ogden Nash. "It isn't a trick."

"The purpose of the writer," Parker felt, "is to say what he feels and sees." And what she felt and saw was the condition of women in an emerging feminist world where there were no longer any firm rules to guide them.

In her gallery of miniatures, she would etch the many aspects of feminine rage; the loneliness of the career woman; the emptiness of women who don't marry but wish to, of those who do marry who find themselves chained to unhappiness and end in divorce, of women with lovers who fail them, of those desperate for love from any source and at any price; and, of course, the men who fuel the flames because they don't *understand.*

In none of this did Dorothy Parker anticipate a happy ending. She simply wrote what she saw and brought to bear—as one critic expressed it—"a disciplined artistry within the framework of a tragic view of life."

Or, rather, a view of death—since it haunted the titles of all her books: *Enough Rope, Sunset Gun, Death and Taxes, Here Lies, Laments for the Living, Not So Deep As a Well,* and, had she ever completed it, her novel *Sonnets in Suicide.*

She was above all a woman of her time, and it's important to remember the greater part of a century later what that time was.

It was considered "fast" for a woman to drink, smoke, bob her hair, roll her stockings, sniff cocaine, dance the Charleston, be overtly promiscuous—and generally act as if anything went.

It was de rigueur to be bitter and cynical, sneer at the romantic, and use the "in lingo," such as "Yea, bo," "Oh, you kid!," "I'll tell the world," "How's the boy?," "Yes, indeedy," "You said a mouthful," and "It's a great life if you don't weaken."

And before we become overly smug, what will future generations make of our "Are you *serious*?," "I'm like . . . ," "*Tell* me about it," "Awesome, and "I mean, Pu-leese!"?

She would always claim that she disliked doing what she did so well—why should anyone "spoil a page with rhymes"?

"And what do you do, Mrs. Parker? Oh, I write. There's a hot job for a healthy woman." She claimed that she would prefer to clean out ferry boats, peddle fish, or be a Broadway chorus boy. Instead, she was—she said—"only a hardworking woman, who writes for a living and hates writing more than anything in the world. . . . I wish I didn't have to work at all. I was made for love, anyway."

She could say it all she wanted but she fooled few. Unlike many writers, she refused to pontificate about her "art," but the occasional unguarded remark would slip through—quite enough to prove that she took her craft very seriously indeed.

"If you are going to write, don't pretend to write it *down*. It's got to be the best you can do and it's the fact that it *is* the best you can do that kills you."

Many people were surprised at how actively she supported young writers. One impecunious young man found a check thrust into his hand with a muttered, "Never mention this to me again. I'm so much in debt myself that this small amount won't make any difference anyway."

"Those who write fantasies . . . are not artists."

"It's a terrible thing to say, but I can't think of good women writers. Of course, calling them women writers is their ruin; they begin to think of themselves that way."

Of an overrated writer, she said, "He's a writer for the ages—for the ages of four to eight."

And she could be very defensive about criticisms of her technical skills. One reviewer once questioned her grammar, which drew the reply, "Maybe it is only I, but conditions are such these days, that if you use studiously correct grammar, people suspect you of homosexual tendencies."

A journalist asked her, "Where is the best place to write?" "In your head."

Why did she write? "Need of money, dear. I'd like to have money. And I'd like to be a good writer. Those two can come together and I hope they will, but if that's too adorable, I'd rather have money. I hate almost all rich people, but I think I'd be darling at it."

"Money can't buy health, but I'd settle for a diamond-studded wheelchair. . . . The two most beautiful words in the English language are—'Check enclosed.'"

At an early age she "fell into writing . . . being one of those awful children who wrote verses." She would always refer to them as "my verses . . . I cannot say poems," and she refused to consider them "real literature." Nonetheless, she was meticulous

> But I am writing little verse,
> As little ladies do.
>
> > ("Song of Perfect Propriety")
>
> Let your rhymes be tinsel treasures,
> Strung and seen and thrown aside
>
> > ("For a Lady Who Must Write Verse")
>
> Ah, could I tempt assorted gents
> As sure as I can Providence,
> A different story I'd rehearse,
> And damned if I'd be writing verse!
>
> > ("The Temptress")

about following the rules of whatever form she attempted—being careful to rhyme the first and third lines of quatrains, for instance.

Light verse was a popular form at the time, and many people who tried their hand at it were careless or ignorant of the rules, much to Dorothy's scorn.

"All you can say is, it didn't do any harm, and it was work that didn't roughen our hands or your mind, just as you can say of knitting."

Later she would come under the literary influence of the popular poet Edna St. Vincent Millay (1892–1950). "Like everybody was then, I was following in the exquisite footsteps . . . unhappily in my own horrible sneakers." One of Miss Millay's poems had the much-quoted lines

> My candle burns at both ends,
> It will not last the night,
> But ah, my foes, and oh, my friends,
> It gives a lovely light.

"That was the style of the day. We were all imitative. We all wandered in after Miss Millay. We were all being dashing and gallant, declaring that we weren't virgins, whether we were or not. Beautiful as she was, Miss Millay did a great deal of harm with her double-burning candles. She made poetry seem so easy that we could all do it. But, of course, we couldn't."

"Then something happened to the light verse writers—especially to the ladies among us. . . . We let it be known that our hearts broke much oftener than the classic once. . . . We sneered in numbers in loping rhythms at the straight and the sharp and the decent."

The theme of most of her work—both then and later—was that men were fickle and that love was a game everyone was destined to lose. Men were pathetic—but women needed them. It was a derivative one, but what she brought to it was a distinctive tone of grim gaiety, sweet sourness. Her words created a carapace around visible vulnerability.

> I shall not see—and don't I know 'em?
> A critic lovely as a poem.
>
>   ("Song in the Worst Possible Taste")
>
> Dark though the clouds, they are silver-lined;
> (This is the stuff that they like to read.)
> If Winter comes, Spring is right behind;
> (This is the stuff that the people need.)
> Smile, and the World will smile back at you;
> Aim with a grin, and you cannot miss;
> Laugh off your blues, and you won't feel blue.
> (Poetry pays when it's done like this.)
>
>   ("The Far-Sighted Muse")

These were essentially personal expressions, and the reader could take them or leave them. When in 1939 she was asked by the Congress of American Writers to talk on poetry, she titled her speech "Sophisticated Verse and the Hell with It!"

Although she continued to write verse intermittently until 1944—and although it remained her most transparently autobiographical form of expression—she concluded that it was not the answer.

"This is a fine thing to be doing, at my age, sitting here making up sissy verses about broken hearts and that tripe at a dollar a line"—when what she really wanted was to be paid for something "in chunks, not drips."

> Show your quick, alarming skill in
> Tidy mockeries of art;
> Never, never dip your quill in
> Ink that rushes from your heart.
>
>   ("For a Lady Who Must Write Verse")

Even so, she remained fiercely protective of what she had achieved:

> Say my love is easy had,
> Say I'm bitten raw with pride,
> Say I am too often sad—
> Still behold me at your side.
> Say I am neither brave nor young,
> Say I woo and coddle care,
> Say the devil touched my tongue—
> Still you have my heart to wear.
> But say my verses do not scan,
> And I get me another man!

("Fighting Words")

"Never tell your dreams. Your poem is an owl that won't bear daylight."

Just before her death she lamented to a friend, "I used to be a poet!"

The short story became her form of choice, but it never came easily to a perfectionist who had found the rigors of meter and rhyme—not to mention the relatively short length—a positive discipline.

She found fiction a difficult and painful process.

"It takes me six months to do a story. I think it out and then write it sentence by sentence (in longhand). . . . I couldn't write five words but that I change seven." She started a writer's notebook, "but I could never remember where I put the damn thing."

She would then type the finished story (and often retype it several times), but even then the problems were not over. "I know so little about the typewriter, I once bought a new one because I couldn't change the ribbon on the one I had."

She was ever watchful—and often envious—of the habits of other writers. "Kathleen Norris said she never wrote a story unless it was fun to do it." At the other end of the literary spectrum, she could easily empathize with "that poor sucker Flaubert rolling round on his floor for three days, looking for the right word."

Almost all her work is written about women—often from the woman's own perspective and, again, frequently autobiographical in content. She would freely admit that she always wrote about herself or people she knew and found herself unable to imagine characters or situations in the abstract. She would take the names of her characters from either the phone book or the obituary columns.

Before long, she had carved out a special niche in "stream-of-consciousness" narrative. You were inside the subject's head or sitting at the next table overhearing a couple in conversation but just too polite to turn around to see their faces. Instead, you could visualize them by what they said and particularly by the way they said it.

Few writers have ever mastered the duplicitous use of dialogue better than Dorothy Parker or the juxtaposition of the spoken word and the thought:

"Oh, yes, it's a waltz. Mind? Why, I'm simply thrilled. I'd love to waltz with you.

"I'd love to waltz with you . . . I'd love to have my tonsils out, I'd love to be in a midnight fire at sea. Well, it's too late now. We're getting under way. . . .

"No, of course it didn't hurt. . . . And it was all my fault. You see, that little step of yours—well, it's perfectly lovely, but it's just a tiny bit tricky to follow at first. Oh, did you work it up yourself? You really did? Well, aren't you amazing? Oh, now I think I've got it. . . .

"I've got several other things, too, including a split shin and a bitter heart. I hate this creature I'm chained to. I hated him the moment I saw his leering, bestial face."

In 1955, she was saying, "I'm not going to do those he said–she said things any more; they're over. . . . I want to do the story that can only be done in the narrative form, and though they're going to scream about the rent, I'm going to do it."

But she did it only once before reverting to the form she had made her own. It was a form she continued to wrestle with, never satisfied that she had mastered it. As late as 1963—when the game was effectively over—she said, "I want to be taken seriously as a short story writer and, by God, I hope to make it."

She made it.

"Write novels, write novels, write novels—that's all they can say. Oh, I do get so sick and tired sometimes."

Certainly her publishers—encouraged by the commercial success of her collections of verse and short stories—could see no reason why the prolific Mrs. Parker couldn't turn that scalpel mind to the longer and even more commercial form. But she could say, "I'm quite incapable of it." She was well aware that, like most of her Round Table friends and contemporaries, she was not a marathon runner but a sprinter. "I'm a short-distance writer."

The nearest she ever got was to participate in an unusual exercise attempted by *Collier's* magazine early in 1925, when nineteen different writers contributed a chapter each to a gangster story called *Bobbed Hair*. The trick was to leave your episode in the most difficult position for your successor to pick up. Dorothy's ended as follows:

"David leaped to his feet in the wildly rocking boat. 'McTish!' he roared across the angry water.

"As he called, the girl had sprung up on the seat beside him. Her arm came swiftly down; there was a curious dull sound, as the revolver butt met his head.

"Slowly and not ungracefully, Mr. David Lacey crumpled up in a heap in the bottom of the boat (*To Be Continued*)."

The summer of 1929 was spent in France, and it's possible she thought a change of ambiance might provide new inspiration. Certainly she weakened enough to promise her Viking publisher, Harold Guinzburg, that she would start on "the novel" to be included in their 1930 list—and take an advance for so doing.

How someone who could take six months on a story thought she could manage a full-length novel in such a short time is hard to imagine—and, of course, she couldn't.

She seems to have tried hard enough to begin with and wrote page after page of what she gave as her working title—*The Events Leading Up to the Tragedy* and then *Sonnets in Suicide; or The Life of John Knox.*

Then the social life closed in on her, and the effort petered out. Visiting Guinzburg—who happened to be in France—for a further advance, she showed him an impressive pile of typed manuscript, omitting to mention that she had padded it out with carbons of old articles and letters from her friends.

The more she persevered, the more painful it became for her to deal with elements of the story that were, by the very nature of the way she wrote, about herself. Realizing that she could never complete her obligation, she panicked and attempted suicide by drinking a bottle of shoe polish. It was not the first, and it would not be the last, of her "cries for help."

Guinzburg and Viking rapidly backed off and published another collection of her short pieces instead. It seemed safer to leave the fragments of *Sonnets in Suicide* in a drawer, where they could not turn into a self-fulfilling prophecy.

The episode, though magnified, was typical of the Parker modus vivendi. Any diversion that took her away from the pain of work was enough. When asked—as she frequently was—why

CHARLES: Thought, dear Mary, has its seasons and mine is at its Springtime. The tender buds are nigh to burst into rich heavy blossoms.
MARY: "Tender buds?" "Rich heavy blossoms?" Charles, what in God's name is all this botany? The excuses I've heard for no work; but "buds" and "blossoms" . . .

(*The Coast of Illyria*)

The cast of *The Coast of Illyria*. Back row, left to right: Edwin Whitner (Coleridge), Clinton Anderson (William Hazlitt), Harold Webster (George Dyer), and Wilson Brooks (Charles Lamb). Front row: John Hudson (Thomas De Quincey), Dorothy Parker, Ross Evans (co-author), and Rebecca Robb (Mary Lamb).

she didn't give up the empty social life and go away and find herself, she would reply, "I can't . . . I don't know how."

Right to the end, she never ceased to respect her God-given talent and would admit to Beatrice Ames Stewart, "I'm betraying it; I'm drinking. I'm not working. I have the most horrendous guilt."

When asked to describe her talent, most people would say that Dorothy Parker was a humorist. She saw herself otherwise.

"I don't want to be classed as a humorist," she would say in the mid-1950s. "It makes me feel guilty. I've never read a good, tough, quotable female humorist, and I never was one myself. I couldn't do it. . . . A 'smart-cracker' they called me and that makes me sick and unhappy. There's a hell of a distance between wisecracking and wit. . . . Wit has truth in it; wisecracking is simply calisthenics with words."

Satire was "another matter" entirely. "They're the big boys. If I'd been called a satirist, there'd be no living with me."

She began to tell everyone that she wished she had never written a humorous line. "Why, I'm not even an amateur humorist," she would protest as early as 1934. "I am very serious, and quite hurt when people laugh at some of my most earnest endeavors." Coming from Dorothy Parker, that sounded like a clever line in itself.

In a preface to a collection of pieces by her friend S. J. Perelman, she would speculate on the subject.

"It is a strange force that compels a writer to be a humorist. It is a strange force, if you care to go back farther, that compels anyone to be a writer at all. . . . The writer's way is rough and lonely, and who would choose it while there are vacancies in more gracious professions, such as, say, cleaning out ferry boats? In all understatement, the author's lot is a hard one, and yet there are those who, in their pride and their innocence, dedicate their careers to writing humorous pieces. Poor dears, the world is stacked against them from the start, for everybody in it has the right to look at their work and say, 'I don't think that's funny.'

"There are quantities of those who, no doubt, in filling out a questionnaire put 'Occupation, humorist.' But their pieces are thin and tidy and timid. They find a little formula and milk it until it moos with pain. They stay with the good old comic symbols so that you won't be upset—the tyrannical offspring, the illiterate business associate, the whooping, devil-may-care old spinster (always reliable), the pitiable inadequacies of a man trying to do a bit of carpentry, the victorious criticisms of the little wife. . . . You have seen those pieces, and they were dead before the sun went down on the day on which they were published.

"I had thought, on starting this composition, that I should define what humor means to me. However, every time I tried to,

I had to go and lie down with a cold wet cloth on my head. Still, here I go. . . . Humor to me, Heaven help me, takes in many things. There must be courage; there must be no awe. There must be criticism, for humor, to my mind, is encapsulated in criticism. There must be a disciplined eye and a wild mind. There must be a magnificent disregard of your reader, for if he cannot follow you, there is nothing you can do about it. There must be some lagniappe in the fact that the humorist has read something written before 1918."

By the mid-1950s—when she was beginning to think retrospectively about a lot of things—she would conclude, "There aren't any humorists any more, except for Perelman. There's no need for them. Perelman must be lonely. . . . It's a question of supply and demand. If we needed them, we'd have them. The new crop of would-be humorists doesn't count. They write about topical topics. Not like Mr. Thurber and Mr. Benchley. Those two were damn well read and, though I hate the word, they were cultured. What sets them apart is that they both had a point of view to express. That is important to all good writing. . . . The writer must be aware of life around him. . . . For most of my reading I go back to the old ones—for comfort. As you get older, you go much further back.

"Humor now is too carefully planned. There is nothing of the old madness Mr. Benchley and some of the others had in my time, no leaping of minds."

Before dismissing her own efforts, she would have done well to go back only as far as Mr. Thurber—her *New Yorker* colleague since 1927—who had written his own apologia in 1951: "I write humor the way a surgeon operates, because it is a livelihood, because I have a great urge to do it . . . and because I have the hope that it may do some good."

"Hooray for Hollywood!"

Hooray for Hollywood!
That screwy bally hooey Hollywood . . .

—Johnny Mercer

Seventy-two suburbs in search of a city.

—Robert Benchley

The only -ism Hollywood believes in is plagiarism.

—Dorothy Parker

Hollywood is the land of yes-men and acqui-yes girls.

—Attributed

The difference between a writer and a Hollywood
writer . . . in Hollywood the writer comes into his
office, takes off his coat, sits at his typewriter, puts the

paper in, puts his fingers on the keys, and waits for the
phone to ring.

—Dorothy Parker

I hate Movies;
They lower my vitality.

—"Movies: A Hymn of Hate"

He it was who made, they say,
Movies what they are today;
This the goal for which he's tried—
Lord, I hope he's satisfied!

"David Wark Griffith"

THE FIRST freelance job Dorothy Parker had after being fired from *Vanity Fair* was writing titles for a movie at a newly opened studio in Mamaroneck, New York. The film was D. W. Griffith's *Remodeling Her Husband*, which was being directed by Griffith's favorite actress, Lillian Gish.

The job lasted precisely one week. To explain a shot in which the hero is having his nails manicured, Dorothy borrowed from Hamlet's speech to Horatio and wrote, "The divinity that shapes our ends." It was not quite what Miss Gish had in mind.

To be fair, she had made her views on the current crop of films quite apparent in one of her "Hymns of Hate":

MOVIES: A HYMN OF HATE

I hate Movies;
They lower my vitality.

There is the Great Spectacle,
Its press-agent admits
That it is the most remarkable picture ever made.
The story is taken from history,

But the scenario writer smoothes things over a little,
And makes Cleopatra Antony's wife,
Or has Salomé marry John the Baptist,
So you can bring the kiddies

There is the High Art Production:
They charge three dollars a seat for it—
That's where they get the "high."
The photography is always tricky;
The actors seem to be enveloped in a dense fog,
And that goes for the plot, too.

Then there is the Picture with Sex Appeal;
The appeal is still unanswered.
The production goes to show
That bad taste, off the screen,
Is still in its infancy.

In 1918, she wrote further of her taste in film: "If I were a movie manager (producer), I would never, under any conceivable circumstance, produce a picture that contained any of the following atrocities: A scene in which a mob chases a fleeing comedian; a close up of the leading lady taken with any kitten, puppy, canary, horse, calf, goldfish, pigeon, deer, monkey or any other fauna whatever; a close up of the leading lady showing large, well-formed tears sliding smoothly down her cheeks; any close up of any leading man and the leading lady, with their backs to the camera and their arms around each others' waist, walking slowly away towards the glowing West; a 'dual role' played by the star who takes the part of two people, one unbelievably noble and the other unspeakably wicked; a comedian whose humor only consists of his avoirdupois; a Western drama in which the town bad man is completely reformed by a little child; any early English hunting scene, taken at the Inn at Forest Hills, Long Island; and lastly, any picture of Mr. Francis X. Bushman."

In the late 1920s, she would describe a movie theater as "an enlarged and magnificently-decorated lethal chamber to me," and what applied to the movies also went for that other intrusive and fashionable medium: radio. She firmly refused to buy a set, and "there is no force great enough to make me."

Her attitude toward the Dream Factory of Hollywood softened appreciably, however, when Mr. Benchley was wooed and went there to begin his celebrated series of short films—some of the earliest films using sustained sound. Much as she admired her friend's achievement, Mrs. Parker found the movie sound tracks crude and annoying. She said she felt like shouting at the screen, "Oh, for heaven's sake, shut up!"

Her own maiden venture, so to speak, was a twenty-five-minute short satire subject for Paramount that she made in 1925 in collaboration with George S. Kaufman, which was in itself surprising since the two were never close. Neither ever spoke about it subsequently, and it sank without trace.

But before she could say "Francis X. Bushman," she was to find herself there in 1929 where so many of the Algonks were already in residence.

"I first went out to Hollywood so long ago that the movie actresses looked flat-chested."

Money was the lure—for once in chunks instead of drips. MGM offered her a three-month screenwriting contract at three hundred dollars a week for what seemed to her to be easy money. Money. She was to be "always hampered by money. . . . It always takes more to live on than what you earn," but this would at least keep the wolf from the Parker door pro tem.

"Why, I could do that with one hand tied behind my back and the other on Irving Thalberg's pulse."

She may have later revised that to "throat" because when she met the studio head, he clearly had no idea who she was or why she was there—hardly surprising when the studio publicity department sent out a release in which she was "the internationally known author of *Too Much Rope*, the popular novel."

(*Enough Rope*, her first collection of verse, had been a critical and popular success just a few years earlier!)

She was given an office. "It was a lovely office but the air was oppressive, and even though I opened the windows and opened the doors, it was still depressing."

She had few visitors, and it was at this time that she felt like telling the man who came to paint her name on the door to letter "Gentlemen" instead. So desperate did things become that when she spotted tourists visiting the studio, she would lean out of her window and shout ,"Let me out. I'm as sane as you are!"

How sane that was might have been open to doubt. She was shown a photograph in a Hollywood newspaper in which three elephants were dressed up as if for a wedding. One wore a clerical collar, one a top hat, and the other a bridal veil. Mrs. Parker looked at it and gave her considered opinion: "I give it six months."

Screenwriting, she was to find, was not what it might appear.

"Nobody can do anything alone. You are given a script that eight people have written from a novel four people have written. You then . . . write dialogue—what a curious word! Well, you know, you can't write dialogue without changing scenes. While you are doing it, eight people back of you are writing beyond you. Nobody is allowed to do anything alone."

If you behaved yourself, occasionally one of the movie moguls might "throw you down a tablet from Mount Sinai."

"You don't need any talents. . . . You need two things—you need skill and you need a fine memory, so if you know what they did in that wild picture in 1938, you're in!"

Over the years, she was to work on many scripts, often uncredited. To the last, she never seems to have mastered the trick the older hands (and hacks) had perfected. You wait until the film is cast and about to start shooting before you involve yourself in the screenplay—that way, the producers can't take you off the credits.

None of her later experiences changed her fundamental conviction.

"I don't believe the films have anything to do with writing except in a crossword-puzzle kind of way. Writing a script is drawing together a lot of ends which can be worked into a moving picture.

"It was a terrible bore, it was a strenuous bore. You sat there and you sat there and you sat there. That's what it was."

Nonetheless, if you agreed to do it, you did it to the best of your ability.

"You aren't writing for the love of it or the art of it or the hell of it or whatever; you are doing a chore assigned to you by your employer and whether or not he might fire you if you did it slackly makes no matter. You've got yourself to face, and you have to live with yourself. You don't—or, at least only in highly exceptional cases—have to live with your producer."

And the experience taught her something else about herself— "one of those eternal, universal truths that serve to make you feel much worse than you did when you started. And that is that no writer, whether he writes from love or for money, can condescend to what he writes. You can't stoop to what you set down on paper. No matter what form it takes, and no matter what the result, and no matter how caustically comic you are about it afterwards, what you did was your best. And to do your best is always hard going."

And, to make matters worse, "Everyone there wrote. I never saw such a thing. The nice man at the gates would write. The producer would write—and that was much worse."

She contributed additional dialogue to a couple of routine films, only to have it rejected as being unsuitable for children. ("God, and how I hate children!") She then contracted to work with Cecil B. DeMille on a film called *Dynamite*.

She was asked to write a theme song for it, and when her submission "Dynamite Man, I Love You" was turned down, it seemed a sensible idea to ask someone to explain what the picture was about.

Getting to see DeMille was "like riding a camel through the eye of a needle," but finally she managed it. DeMille took her through a convoluted plot, which involved the wrongly accused hero sitting in his prison cell with only his guitar for company—and, of course, he'd need a song to sing, which is where Dorothy's contribution was to come in.

At a comparative loss for words, she could only mutter how the details were "just staggering."

"Ah, yes," DeMille replied, "zebras in *The King of Kings*," as if that explained everything.

It was only on a subsequent visit that she had the temerity to ask him where the zebras came in. He explained that they were pulling the chariots of Mary Magdalene. Unfortunately, when they kicked, their legs were inclined to break.

"Of course," said the sympathetic Mrs. Parker, "I should have known that."

"After some weeks I ran away. I could not stand it any more. I just sat in a cell-like office and did nothing. The life was expensive and the thousands of people I met were impossible. They never seemed to behave naturally, as if all their money gave them a wonderful background they could never stop to marvel over. I would imagine the Klondike like that—a place where people rush for gold. . . . I didn't get there in time . . . when there wasn't a party that was any good unless there were two dead bodies on the lawn."

As she took the train back to New York, she would reflect on her experience. She had known she would hate Hollywood, if only because of the palm trees, "the ugliest vegetable God created," and as for MGM, "Metro-Goldwyn-Merde" would be a better name for that "shit heap. . . . I hoped the whole industry would collapse. . . . It looks, it all feels as if it had been invented by a Sixth Avenue peep-show man."

But, of course, the industry was to have the last laugh. As one executive explained, there were many expatriates who liked to use Mrs. Parker's favorite appellation for Hollywood when they arrived—then stayed to eat it.

MRS. LATHAM: How do you like California, Miss Wykoff?
STELLA: I hate oranges.

(*The Ice Age*)

Dorothy Parker was not one of those who stayed, but she did return. In 1934, she married Alan Campbell, who persuaded her that they could conquer Hollywood by offering themselves as a writing "team." Mrs. Parker-Campbell—undeterred by the studio executive's comment—was all for "filing the whole thing under Horseshit," but Campbell persisted and negotiated a dual contract for them with Paramount: two hundred and fifty dollars a week for him and a thousand for Dorothy. When they proved successful, the joint fee was raised considerably. Although she did not expect the work to be any more rewarding, at least it would help reduce their debt ("Dottie's dowry").

There were, however, aspects of the contract she found less than appealing: "I see . . . that I am to work for Mr. Lee Tracy, the gentleman who micturated over Mexico. He does that, it appears, when he is not amused. I am planning to wear a shower-curtain to work."

After a while she would admit, "It's all right. No art but you can make a little money and clear up that national debt. . . . We're up to 1912 now."

Perhaps it was marriage that helped her adjust better to her physical surroundings, at least this time around.

"Aside from the work, which I hate like holy water, I love it here. There are any number of poops about, of course, but so are there in New York—or, as we call it, The Coast—and the weather's better here. I love having a house, I love its being pretty wherever you look." (She had, presumably, learned to love the palms.) "You could have the most remarkable house. You could have a pool, if you wished. I don't swim. My goodness, you could have so many things, and you said to yourself while you were there—

'For heaven's sake, I might as well live as good as I can while I have to be here.'"

Settling in, though, was not without its problems. They found a house they wanted to rent, but then the real estate agent found out who and what they were. In a letter to Woollcott, she explained the outcome, which was pure Hollywood.

"'Writers,' he said, 'And connected with the movies, too. No, thank you. We can't have that kind of people in this house.' You see the place is the property of Miss Ruth Etting and her former husband, known as Colonel Moe the Gimp. It is the house in which the embittered Gimp had shot Miss Etting's boyfriend through the bowels when he sneaked in and caught the boyfriend and Miss E in what the newspapers call an embrace. To me the story was lifted into the upper brackets by the fact that also present in the room was the Gimp's daughter by a former marriage. She had apparently drawn up a chair to watch. When the Gimp entered, she was so incensed at the interruption, she ran out of the room and returned with a gun to shoot Daddy with. But Daddy got it away from her and—well, so there he was with a gun in his hand and there was the boyfriend, right there, so—

"Well, anyway, that's the house from which we're barred, because we're writers."

A few such incidents caused her to christen the place "Sodom-in-the-Sun . . . Poughkeepsie with Palms," and one day a single image crystallized the whole thing for her.

"I was coming down a street in Beverly Hills and I saw a Cadillac about a block long, and out of the side window was a wonderfully slinky mink, and an arm, and at the end of the arm a hand in a white suede glove wrinkled at the wrist, and in the hand was a bagel with a bite out of it."

Her arrival was like a reunion of the Round Table. She was given an office at Paramount. "A bit of cardboard with my name inked on it was tacked on the door. A soirée started at once . . . and lasted for several days. Men of letters, bearing gin bottles, arrived. Bob Benchley, halooing with laughter, as if he had come from the land of Punch and Judy, was there, and the owlish-eyed satirist, Donald Ogden Stewart, beaming as at a convention of March Hares. One night at a flossy party Don appeared on the dance floor in a long overcoat. 'That's silly and showing off to dance in an overcoat,' said the great lady of the films in his arms. 'Please take it off.' Don did. He had nothing on underneath."

As in New York, it was the social life that brought Mrs. Parker to life and sharpened her verbal reflexes. One night, the inevitable party was going on in her suite at the Chateau Marmont. In the room immediately overhead was her other Viking publisher, George Oppenheimer. Suddenly, there was a loud crash from above: "Pay no attention. It's only George dropping another name."

Their "collaboration" would amount to Alan blocking out a scene while Dorothy endlessly knitted. When he had finished, she would add amusing dialogue.

"Alan and I are working on a little opera which was originally named *Twenty-Four Hours by Air*, but it has been kicking around the studio for a long time, during which aerial transportation has made such progress that is now called *Eleven Hours by Air*. By the time we are done, the title is to be, I believe, *Stay Where You Are* (When the film finally appeared it was, in fact, called *One Hour Late*.)

"Before this, we were summoned to labor on a story of which we were told only, 'Now we don't know yet whether the male lead will be played by Tullio Carminati or Bing Crosby. So just sort of write it with both of them in mind.' Before that we were assigned the task of taking the sex out of *Sailor Beware*. . . . They read our script and went back to the original version. The catch for the movies, it seemed, was that hinge of the plot where the sailor bets he will make the girl. They said that was dirty. But would they accept our change, that triumph of ingenuity where the sailor just bets he will make another sailor? Oh, no! Sometimes I think they don't know *what* they want." By "they" she meant the producers—her opinion of them in general was not high.

Of MGM's Hunt Stromberg, "If a doctor should tap one of his knees, probing for a reflex, both his feet would fly into the air at once, knocking off his shoes." Of another, "He hasn't got enough sense to bore assholes in wooden hobbyhorses."

One who had perhaps more sense than was good for him was the young and newly independent David O. Selznick. Dorothy and Alan were contracted to him to work on the 1937 *A Star Is Born*, a film to be described by the *New York Times* as "the most accurate mirror ever held before the glittering, tinseled, trivial, generous, cruel and ecstatic world that is Hollywood."

Dorothy Parker described a typical Selznick meeting in a letter to Alexander Woollcott.

"So last week the board of directors of Selznick Pictures, Inc. had a conference. The four members of the board sat around a costly table in an enormously furnished room, and each was supplied with a pad of scratch paper and a pencil. After the conference was over, a healthily curious young employee (*sic*) of the company went to look at the scratch pads. He found:

"Mr. David Selznick had drawn a seven-pointed star, before that, a six-pointed star, and before that again, a row of vertical lines like a little picket fence.

"Mr. John Whitney's pad had nothing at all on it.

"Dr. Gianinni, the noted California banker, had written over and over, in a long neat column, the word 'tokas,' which is Yiddish for 'arse.'

"And Mr. Mervan (*sic*) Cooper, the American authority on Technicolor, had printed on the middle of his page RIN-TIN-TIN.

"The result of the conference was that hereafter the company would produce twelve pictures a year instead of six.

"I don't know, I just thought you might wish to be assured that Hollywood does not change."

Despite her skepticism, *A Star Is Born* was a considerable success, and she and Alan received an Oscar nomination for that year. She claimed that she never saw the finished film: "I went to see it all alone for a few minutes." Nonetheless, it surely strengthened her underlying conviction—rarely expressed—that "people, once given the chance, would be as partial to good pictures as they once were to bad ones."

Oh come, my love, and join with me
The oldest infant industry.
Come seek the bourne of palm and pearl,
The lovely land of Boy-Meets-Girl,
Come grace this lotus-laden shore,
This Isle of Do-What's-Done-Before,
Come, curb the new, and watch the old win,
Out where the streets are paved with Goldwyn.

> ("The Passionate Screen Writer to His Love")

Even more surrealistic than the encounter with Selznick was the relationship with legendary producer Samuel Goldwyn, who paid the couple $5,200 a week as opposed to their average $2,000.

In the days of the major studios, a relative handful of people like Goldwyn—usually first-generation Jewish émigrés from other, unrelated industries—dictated the taste of Hollywood movies and pitched it to the lowest common denominator for the "melting pot" society they were providing with "product."

"Out in Hollywood, where the streets are paved with Goldwyn, the word 'sophisticate' means, very simply, 'obscene.' A sophisticated story is a dirty story. Some of that meaning has wafted eastward and got itself mixed up in the present definition. So that a 'sophisticate' means: one who dwells in a tower made of a Dupont substitute for ivory and holds a glass of flat champagne in one hand and an album of dirty postcards in the other."

Dorothy and Alan were assigned to *You Can Be Beautiful*, an already well-thumbed property about an Elizabeth Arden kind of character. Surely Dorothy could come up with a twist. How about making her a perfectly happy plain girl who turns into a discontented beauty?

At this Goldwyn exploded. This was precisely why Dorothy Parker, despite her great talent, wasn't more commercially successful—she refused to give the public what they wanted.

"But, Mr. Goldwyn, people don't *know* what they want until you give it to them."

"Nonsense," the mogul replied, "people want a happy ending."

"I know this will come as a shock to you, Mr. Goldwyn, but in all history, which has held billions and billions of human beings, not a single one ever had a happy ending."

Exit Mrs. Parker.

Goldwyn threw up his hands in despair. "Does anybody know what the hell that woman was talking about?"

Later they were providing additional dialogue for Lillian Hellman's *The Little Foxes.* In the middle of the night, she was awakened by a phone call from Goldwyn.

"I've seen the rushes and that picture's communistic. It's communism pure and simple, I tell you!"

"But Sam, the story's set in the early 1900s. There wasn't any Communism then."

"Thank God!"

But perhaps the relationship was best summed up by this exchange:

GOLDWYN: Do you really say all those things which the
    papers report you say?
PARKER: Do *you?*

At that time she told an interviewer, "I say hardly any of those clever things that are attributed to me. I wouldn't have time to earn a living if I said all those things."

She was to claim that of all the films she ever worked on, *The Little Foxes* was the only one that ever satisfied her—"aside from the check every week." And when Goldwyn didn't pick up their option, a million-dollar-plus nest egg rode off into the sunset.

Her reputation continued to haunt her in Hollywood. Newspaper magnate William Randolph Hearst—"the world's greatest son of a bitch" and the model for Orson Welles's

1941 *Citizen Kane*—built an ostentatious bungalow for his mistress Marion Davies with a statue of the Madonna at the entrance. A verse appeared in a rival paper with which Mrs. Parker was credited:

> Upon my honor
> I saw a Madonna
> Standing in a niche
> Above the door
> Of a prominent whore
> Of a prominent son of a bitch.

She indignantly denied authorship—not on grounds of taste but because she would never stoop to rhyming "honor" with "Madonna." She also recalled that as an actress, Miss Davies had two expressions: "joy and indigestion."

Hollywood in the late 1930s and early 1940s seemed to be full of that other species of émigré, the expatriate British actor. Mrs. Parker found their overly precise pronunciation increasingly irritating. When Herbert Marshall—freshly returned from the United Kingdom—was consulting his diary and talking about his busy "shedyule," she looked up from her knitting long enough to remark, "If you don't mind my saying so, I think you're full of skit."

Her observations of people's personal appearance were predictably barbed. Basil Rathbone she considered to be nothing but "two profiles pasted together"; a well-known gay English actor "simply buggers description"; and when an ambitious young actor whose own profile was sadly out of kilter confided his hopes for stardom, she replied ingenuously and encouragingly, "Oh, they've been *searching* for a new Cary Grant!"

She even played a bit part in one of her own films before she left Hollywood. One of her better screenplays was undoubtedly Alfred Hitchcock's 1942 industrial espionage ("spies and lies") thriller *Saboteur*.

Hitchcock made it a point to make a token appearance in each of his films, and he and Parker may be seen as the couple in a car driving past when the hero (Robert Cummings) is apparently manhandling the heroine (Priscilla Lane). Mrs. Parker gave herself the one line, but it is typical. Observing the struggling couple, she remarks, "Oh, they must be *very* much in love!"

As early as 1940, she was persuading Alan to begin to fold their Hollywood tents. She insisted on selling their house. When she told him that "there descends on the house in the later afternoon what I would call a suicide light," that was enough to persuade him.

But leaving the place for good wasn't as easy as all that. In 1947, they were back working for Universal-International on an original screenplay, *Smash Up: The Story of a Woman*, which won them their second Oscar nomination—though, again, they didn't win. It was also the year that Dorothy Parker divorced Alan Campbell.

But even divorce didn't work for her, and in 1950 they remarried, though for much of the next few years they lived apart.

This time it would be fine. Alan returned to Hollywood, and eventually Dorothy rejoined him there for what proved to be their last hurrah.

They lived not in some grand mansion high in the Hollywood Hills but in a small wooden house in the suburbs. The address was Norma Place, but Mrs. Parker immediately rechristened it "Peyton Place West."

They had neighbors of varying degrees of fame and, in her critical eyes, eccentricity. There was starlet Tuesday Weld ("Have you met Tuesday Weld's mother, Wednesday yet?"—not one of her better lines), the touchy gay neighbor ("There he goes, tossing his Shirley Temple curls"), and the aging actress Estelle Winwood, who had once been Alan's lover ("And she was creaking even then"). When told that Miss Winwood had been cast in the film of *Camelot*, Parker said, "Playing a battlement, no doubt?"

And there was the other male neighbor who invited them all in to admire the portrait of himself he had just commissioned. It showed him full frontal nude with his genitalia somewhat enhanced. After contemplating it for a while, Dorothy said admiringly, "It's so real, you almost feel he could speak to you, don't you?"

And then, when Alan died in 1963, it was finally and irrevocably over. In fact, it had been over for some time. Her outspokenness on political matters from the 1930s on had caused her to be "blacklisted" in the neurotic atmosphere of the early 1950s. Dorothy Parker was never convicted and imprisoned—as a number of her colleagues were—but she was effectively unemployable.

And so she returned to New York for good. "I get up every morning and want to kiss the pavement."

She would frequently reflect on her "fifteen years on and off" Hollywood experience, despite the fact that "I can't talk about Hollywood. It was a horror to me when I was there and it's a horror to look back on. I can't imagine how I did it. When I got away from it, I couldn't even refer to the place by name. 'Out there,' I called it. . . .

"[It] smells like laundry. The beautiful vegetables taste as if they were raised in trunks, and at those wonderful supermarkets you find that the vegetables are all wax. The flowers out there smell like dirty, old dollar bills. Sure, you make money writing on the Coast and God knows you earn it, but that money is like so much compressed snow. It goes so fast it melts in your hand.

"I do not feel that I am participating in a soft racket (and what the hell, by the way, is a *hard* racket?) when I am writing for the screen. Nor do I want to be part of any racket, hard or soft or three-and-a-half minutes. I have never in my life been paid so much, either. . . . But I can look my God and my producer—whom I do not, as do many, confuse with each other—in the face, and say that I have earned every cent of it."

"You Might as Well Live": Drink, Suicide, and Other Forms of Death and Destruction

Razors pain you;
Rivers are damp;
Acids stain you;
And drugs cause cramp.
Guns aren't lawful;
Nooses give;
Gas smells awful;
You might as well live.

—"Resumé"

There's little in taking or giving,
There's little in water or wine;
This living, this living, this living,
Was never a project of mine.

—"Coda"

Sorrow is tranquility remembered in emotion.

—Dorothy Parker

Dorothy Parker yearned her living.

—Alexander Woollcott

It costs me never a stab nor squirm
To tread by chance upon a worm.
"Aha, my little dear," I say
"Your clan will pay me back one day."

—"Thought for a Sunshiny Morning"

DEATH WAS to become a leitmotif in Dorothy Parker's life—so much so that it became almost a joke. And since it was a joke that most of her real friends did not appreciate, she enjoyed it even more. Only Mr. Benchley could strike the appropriate tone. Visiting her in hospital after a suicide attempt, he remonstrated, "Dottie, if you don't stop this sort of thing, you'll make yourself sick."

Whether the premature death of two "mothers" gave her a morbid fascination with the subject or whether this was something inherent in her nature is open to question. Certainly, she idealized her real mother and brooded over her death.

The cool of linen calms my bed,
And there at night I stretch my length
And envy no one but the dead.

("Story of Mrs. W—")

Drawing by Lynne Carey.

Twenty-five years later, she was still brooding. "The dead are all so good!" The "wistful dead" were also "pompous":

The earth is cool across their eyes;
They lie there quietly.
But I am neither old nor wise,
They do not welcome me.

("The White Lady")

It became an early preoccupation in her life to anticipate the end of it. At various times she would compose her own epitaph— "Pardon My Dust," "This Is on Me," and "If You Can Read This, You Are Standing Too Close."

"I want to be buried in a shroud made of unpaid bills from Valentina. . . . I had long ago made my design for what was to become of me when the Reaper had swung his scythe through my neck. . . . I was to be cremated after death—at least, I always trusted it would be after death. I even left instructions to this effect in my will, a document that might otherwise be written in a large, school-girl backhand on the head of a pin. . . . Now I want to be left as approximately is, so that I may be buried in a prominent place on a traveled thoroughfare through a wildly popular cemetery. Above me I want a big white stone. . . . I like to think of my shining tombstone. It gives me, as you might say, something to live for."

Although after writing her will, the least she could now do, she said, was to die.

The death of close friends—which came thick and fast in her later years—depressed her greatly. As early as 1945, when Benchley died suddenly of a brain tumor, she murmured, almost to herself, "Isn't it a bit presumptuous of us to be alive now that Mr. Benchley is dead?"

Her favorite perfume—which she had imported from Clyclax of London—was tuberose, a heavy scent used by undertakers to mask the smell of a corpse. In her case, she used it to hide the pervasive evidence of alcohol.

Drink was a preoccupation, amounting to an occupation, with the Algonks and a vast proportion of the 1920s socialites—not least because it was illegal. "Bootleg hooch," as it was affectionately called, rotted many an articulate liver during the years of Prohibition (1919–1933). Nor did three packs of Chesterfields a day help.

Mrs. Parker—in her true autobiographical fashion—documented her own alcoholic odyssey in her O. Henry prize–winning story, "Big Blonde":

"She commenced drinking alone, little short drinks all through the day. . . . Alone, it blurred sharp things for her. She lived in a haze of it. Her life took on a dream-like quality. Nothing was astonishing. . . . She was never noticeably drunk and seldom nearly sober. It required a large daily allowance to keep her misty-minded. Too little, and she was achingly melancholy."

When Parker was alone, she complained of "the howling horrors." Scotch was her drink of choice, and she would often define her own mood as "Scotch mist." When trying to cut down, she would switch to highballs, "awfully weak; just cambric Scotch." When things got out of hand, she would excuse it as "just the effects of that new Scotch of mine which, friends tell me, must have been specially made by the Borgias." "White Hearse" was her name for cheap generic Scotch. Gin, fortunately, made her sick.

Asked what she would like for breakfast—"Just something light and easy to fix. How about a dear little whiskey sour? Make it a double, while you're up." The phrase became so associated with her that it eventually turned up in an advertising campaign for Grant's Stand Fast—"While you're up, get me a Stand Fast."

There has yet to be evidence that heavy drinkers are any better than the amateurs at avoiding the dreaded hangover. Mrs. Parker would often suffer from one "so impressive it should be referred to as 'we' . . . it ought to be in the Smithsonian under glass." She called the extreme version of the condition "the rams."

"The rams, as I hope you need never find out for yourself, are much like the heebie-jeebies, except that they last longer, strike deeper, and are, in general, fancier. The illness was contracted on

Thursday night at an informal gathering, and I am convinced it may be directly traced to the fact that I got a stalk of bad celery at dinner. It must have been bad celery, because you can't tell me that two or three sidecars, some champagne at dinner, and a procession of mixed Benedictine-and-Brandies, taking seven hours to pass a given point, are going to leave a person in that state where she is afraid to turn around suddenly lest she see a Little Mean Man about eighteen inches tall, wearing a yellow slicker and roller-skates. Besides the continued presence of the Little Mean Man, there are such minor symptoms as loss of correct knee action, heartbreak, an inability to remain either seated or standing, and a constant sound in the ears as of far-off temple bells. These, together with a readiness to weep at any minute and a racking horror of being left alone, positively identify the disease as the rams. Bad celery will give you the rams quicker than anything else. You want to look out for it. There's a lot of it around."

"Every time I took my head off the pillow, it would roll under the bed. This isn't my head I've got on now. I think this is something that used to belong to Walt Whitman."

A brief pre-Hollywood sojourn in Denver with her then actor husband, Alan, proved tedious, but it did provide one alcoholic insight. "Drinking here is quite an interesting experiment, because of the altitude. Two cocktails, and you spin on your ass."

Parker's doctor warned her on one occasion that if she didn't stop drinking, she would be dead within a month. "Promises, promises!" On another he told her he didn't like her kidneys. "I don't like your nose."

Benchley persuaded her to consult Alcoholics Anonymous. She returned to report that she had been and found the whole organization perfectly wonderful. "So are you going to join?" Benchley asked. "Certainly not. They wanted me to stop *now*."

Age was another concern. Shakespeare might write as much as he liked about age not withering nor custom staling a woman's infinite variety, but Dorothy Parker wasn't buying it. When in 1944 she hit her fiftieth birthday, she knew he was full of her favorite word.

"This is it, you know, baby. This is the one that does it. You have said farewell to the thirties for the tenth and last time. Now you face it, baby. Now you take it smack in the teeth, baby. Quote, baby, unquote.

"A fine lot of good that ever did, trying to lie about your age. The most you could plausibly knock off was a couple of years, and what's a couple of sandspits to an archipelago? Perhaps if you had moved to a strange city and given it out that you had had a terribly tragic life, spent mostly in the tropics, you might have been able to subtract something worthwhile.

"Well, all right, Middle Age. You've been hanging around here for ten years. Take your foot out of the door and come on in. . . . No—please wait a minute. . . . Please, just another minute. . . . I can't quite. . . .

"It's the word 'middle.' Any phrase it touches becomes the label of the frump; middle of the road, middle class, middle age. If only you could leap those dreary decades and land up in the important numbers. There is chic to seventy, elegance to eighty.

"People ought to be one of two things, young or old. No; what's the good of fooling? People ought to be one of two things, young or dead.

Drink and dance and laugh and lie;
Love, the reeling midnight through,
For tomorrow we may die!
(But, alas, we never do.)

("The Flaw in Paganism")

If wild my breast and sore my pride,
I bask in dreams of suicide;
If cool my heart and high my head,
I think "How lucky are the dead!"

("Rhyme against Living")

"Oh, come in Middle Age, come in, come in! Come close to me, give me your hand, let me look in your face. . . . Oh. . . . Is that what you are really like? . . . Oh, God help me . . . help me."

There were at least half a dozen recorded attempts at suicide and probably several more. How serious they were is hard to tell.

The first was in January 1923 with her husband Eddie's razor. When told—presumably jokingly!—that she should have cut deeper, she responded with one of her Inept Eddie lines—"The trouble was Eddie hadn't even been able to sharpen his own razors."

Even so, she took care to order room service before doing so. On another occasion involving an overdose of sleeping pills, she threw the glass through the bedroom window, thereby ensuring the strong likelihood of someone coming to investigate the incident. Next to Scotch—and often with it—sleeping pills were an addiction with her. She took them, she said, "in a big bowl with sugar and cream."

Serious attempts—or cries for help? Only her psychiatrist would know for sure, and she would have run a mile rather than consult one and be told to do what she had no intention of doing.

Other people's suicides held no interest for her. When told that an ex-lover had blown his brains out in an airport, she is supposed to have said, "What else could he do?" And then to add—in a remark that would be echoed in the one she was to make after Alan's own sudden death—"There goes my whipping boy; I hope he left his whips behind."

Certainly, the theater of her *own* suicide put her center stage with her friends—until they eventually tired of the act.

When Benchley visited her in hospital the first time, he found her in an oxygen tent. "May I please have a flag for my tent?" she asked. He was not amused.

Hospital stays were a return to the womb. Someone was there to look after her—more or less. Woollcott once visited her in "Bedpan Alley," only to have her ring the bell for the nurse. Why had she done that? Was something wrong? It was, she explained, the only way to assure them of "forty-five minutes of absolute privacy."

The only problem with a hospital stay was the inevitable bill. The first was paid by a loan—which she eventually repaid—from silent screen star John Gilbert ("a dear but he never wants to go to bed"). Dorothy would frequently have to depend on the kindness of friends, if not strangers, being, she insisted, "poorer than poverty itself" because of her profligate lifestyle. This was something her friends completely failed to understand since she received generous advances and royalties from her publishers. What they did not realize until after her death was her habit of throwing her checks to the back of a drawer and forgetting all about them. When she died, some $20,000 worth of them was found there.

Her mind, she said, was "a little den of demons," and there is little doubt that had she been able and willing to consult a specialist today, he would have diagnosed her condition as manic depression and put her on a course of antidepressants. In the Age of Prozac, would we have experienced the tortured brilliance of the Age of Dorothy Parker, or would we have had to settle for the well-mannered "little verse" of a sedated little lady?

Songs and Plays:
An Intermission

" DOROTHY PARKER—SONGWRITER" and "Dorothy Parker—Playwright" are not concepts that spring readily to mind, though, in fact, she wrote a number of both over the years. She never regarded herself as being particularly musical and as a performer restricted herself to playing the triangle at the occasional ad hoc musical evenings at the apartment of painter Neysa McMein.

Playing music was one thing, but writing *lyrics*, as she confided to her *Vanity Fair* readers in a 1919 article, was something absolutely anyone could do "in your spare time, in the privacy of your own room," and was infinitely preferable to "selling used cars."

She was talking—she hastened to add—about songs for musical comedies, which were totally interchangeable. Beginners should avoid the "intimate" musicals, such as those currently being devised by Messrs. Wodehouse, Bolton, and Kern. Many of their lyrics "have had words of three and four syllables, while several of them contained references to Caesar, Cleopatra, Galahad and like obscure characters." No, "your lyrics should appeal to the man of average intellect . . . and let it go at that. . . .

"It doesn't matter in the least about the plot of the comedy that your lyrics will adorn. Any set of lyrics will fit in any musical show—that's the trick of it. As they are all on such timely topics as love, moonlight, roses, Spring and you, you, you, they can be worked in any place and any time. . . .

"In case you don't happen to remember exactly the songs in the last dozen or so musical comedies, here are a few general rules to follow, if you want to be a successful lyricist.

"In the first place, never bother about the opening choruses. Let the assembled super-numeraries sing any words that they can think of. No one will pay any attention to them, anyway. During the first one, the ushers will be showing late theatre-parties to their seats, and explaining to the people already in those seats that their tickets were for the night before last. During the opening choruses of the following acts, all those gentlemen who just stepped out to find out the right time will be laboriously and apologetically climbing back into their mid-row places. All this will cause such a pleasant bustle among the audience that only experienced lip-readers could tell what those on the stage were singing. So you don't have to worry about that. Just so long as they all end together, very high, on something like 'Hurray!' or 'Be gay!'—or 'Some night!'—or anything in that spirit, all will be well.

"It is always advisable to get the big song hit in early, and then repeat it at fifteen minute intervals during the show. Have each member of the cast sing it at least once, let the orchestra play it between the acts and as an exit number, and have it frequently rendered on bells, secreted in different parts of the house. *Make* the audience like it.

"It will, of course, be about love. What else is there to write about? Always remember that it is unethical to use plain 'dove,' or ungarnished 'above,' as a rhyme for 'love'; 'dove' must only be used in 'cooing dove,' while 'above' may be employed in one of two ways—either 'true as the skies above,' or 'I'll swear by the stars above.' In this song, as in every other, always strive to make rhymes more intricate than is absolutely essential. When in doubt about rhyming words, always take the more difficult way—that is the only rule you need remember.

"The song hit you will find, will develop somewhat along these lines:

> I've traveled all around the world,
>   In every sort of clime.
> I've met most every kind of girl,
>   And some I thought were fine.
> But since I first loved you, I'd like
>   To always settle down,
> Because, from morn till late at night,
>   Love makes the world go round.

> Chorus:
> For love is always love,
>   Most everybody knows.
> I'll be true as skies above,
>   Like the sunshine is true to the rose.
> Yes, love is always love—
>   Just ask the cooing dove,
> In all sorts of weather,
>   Love lingers forever,
> For love is always love.

"As a finale to your first act, you must work in a song in which the entire troupe is going somewhere. They must always be on the point of starting for some other place, as the first curtain falls—this is essential. It brings out that free unhampered spirit that people in musical comedies always have. . . .

"No, one of the principals just says, 'Let's go to Samoa—how about it, girls?' and the cast simply rushes out into the wings, gets its suitcases and troops back again, all ready to start.

"The going-away song is rendered by a lady in a traveling costume composed chiefly of field-glasses. The chorus goes rather like this:

> I'm on my way to Samoa,
> To sit on that beautiful shore.
>> Though everyone sighs,
>> I am saying goodbye.
> For I'm sailing the sea o'er to Samoa.

"In the second act, always bring in a specialty song. It is a novel conceit to have the *ingénue* come out in pink rompers, and lisp a ballad of sweet innocent childhood. Remember that all children's songs must be about sex problems—this is their only accepted subject. Here's your chance to let yourself go on the lyrics:

> I've a little baby brother,
>> We have had him most a year.
> Both my father and my mother
>> Say the stork has brought him here.
> But I know just where I'm at,
>> Though I've never been to school.
> If they think I fall for that—
>> Gee, they must think I'm a fool!

> Chorus:
> I know a thing or two, you bet,
>> Though I don't make a splurge.
> Though I am hardly seven yet,
>> I've felt the cosmic urge!
> That stork stuff bores me most to tears,
>> It's simply too absurd—
> Why, I've known for the last four years
>> That there ain't no such bird.

"In the last act, of course, there has to be a patriotic number. Something has to be done to use up all the uniforms,

American flags, and back drops showing the entire army in action. The managers bought up the entire market of these properties and then the war went and stopped on them. Those things must be used! A song like this will stop the show:

> Now our boys are back once more,
> For the conflict now is o'er.
> To their homes once more they come
> After vanquishing the Hun.
> Over there, the fighting's over,
> They are coming back to mother,
> Guns no more upon their shoulders.
> All are welcoming our soldiers!
>
> Chorus:
> They are back to the land of Liberty,
> After saving the world for democracy.
> They have sailed o'er the foam
> And they're coming back home,
> To the old Red, White and Blue.
> While the brass band plays the "Marseillaise,"
> We will welcome every man
> Who has fought for Uncle Sam
> For they saved the world for I and you.

And then she proceeded to take her own advice.

The first Parker lyric that can be verified was for an amateur revue put on by the Round Tablers on April 30, 1922. Inspired by the hit show *Chauve-Souris*, they devised *No, Sirree!* (The exclamation mark was obligatory for musical shows of the period.) It was billed as "An Anonymous Entertainment by the Vicious Circle of the Hotel Algonquin."

By all accounts, both the content and the performances were amateurish in the extreme—the only exception being Robert Benchley's monologue "The Treasurer's Report" (which was *meant* to sound so). On the strength of it, Irving Berlin (who had conducted the orchestra) and his partner Sam Harris signed Benchley up for their own new *Music Box Revue* and started him off on what was to become his alternative and lucrative career as a performer.

Mrs. Parker's contribution was to write the lyrics of a song called "The Everlastin' Ingenue Blues," which was sung by Robert Sherwood and a chorus line that included Tallulah Bankhead and Helen Hayes. (Sherwood was to adapt the idea of the amateur hoofer for Alfred Lunt years later in his 1936 play *Idiot's Delight.*) It ran, in part,

> GIRLS: We've got the blues,
> We've got the blues—
> We believe we said before—
> We've got the blues . . .
> We are little flappers, never growing up,
> And we've all of us been flapping
> Since Belasco was a pup . . .
>
> 1ST GIRL: I'm an ingénue and I've got the blues . . .
> 2ND GIRL: . . . as anyone can plainly see . . .
> 3RD GIRL: Because an ingénue
> Must promise to . . .
> 4TH GIRL: . . . imprison her virginity.
> 1ST GIRL: I checked my maidenhead
> In my producer's bed . . .
> 2ND GIRL: Oh gosh, I guess the joke's on me!

No, Sirree! was, fortunately, always intended as a one-performance phenomenon and pleased the participants, if no one else. It must also have given its occasional lyricist a taste for the form since we find her two years later contributing to another not-much-longer-lived show devised by Algonks George S. Kaufman and Herman Manckiewicz, *Round the Town*, with two songs—"It's Good for You to Exercise Your Mind" (music by Arthur Samuels) and "Romeo, Juliet, Johnny and Jane" (with music by the legendary Victor Herbert).

None of those lyrics appears to be extant, so the first *published* Parker lyric was the one she wrote for DeMille's 1929 film *Dynamite*. Having had her first, tongue in cheek (?) submission, "Dynamite Man, I Love You," turned down, she and composer Jack King came up with the following:

HOW AM I TO KNOW?
(Sung by Russ Columbo)

Delicate moon,
Over the silent lane,
Lighten the dark, show me the answer plain,
Here in my breast, wakens my heart,
When will it rest? Why does it start?
Delicate moon, what is this lovely pain,
For . . .
Oh,
How am I to know
If it's really love
That found its way here?
Oh,
How am I to know,
Will it linger on and leave me then?
I dare not guess at this strange happiness,
For . . .

Oh,
How am I to know,
Can it be that love
Has come to stay here,
Stay here?

Glittering star,
Low in the misty blue,
Brighten my dream, tell me at last it's true,
How shall I learn, but from above?

Where shall I turn, looking for love?
Glittering star, maybe I always knew,
But . . .

Oh,
How am I to know . . . etc

In 1934, she wrote a song with music by Ralph Rainger:

I WISHED ON THE MOON

Ev'ry night was long and gloomy,
Shadows gathered in the air.
No one ever listened to me.
No one wondered did I care.
None in all the world to love me,
None to count the stars that hung.
Then the moon came out above me
And I saw that it was young.

I wished on the moon
For something I never knew,
Wished on the moon
For more than I ever knew.
A sweeter rose,
A softer sky,
An April day
That would not dance
Away

I begged of a star
To throw me a beam or two,
Wished on a star
And asked for a dream or two.
I looked for ev'ry loveliness,
It all came true.
I wished on the moon for you.

Then a long silence until—in 1956—she became involved with a project that eventually sank under the weight of the collective talents involved in it.

Voltaire's satirical novel *Candide* (1759) was at the heart of it with a book by Lillian Hellman, score by Leonard Bernstein, and lyrics by poet Richard Wilbur, critic James Agee, lyricist John Latouche—and Dorothy Parker.

"I had only one lyric in it. It didn't work out very well. . . . Thank God I wasn't there while it was going on. There were too many geniuses involved, you know."

She was to blame Bernstein for the fact that the show didn't gel. The professional polymath had to have a hand in every aspect of it. "Lenny Bernstein has to do everything . . . and to do it better than anybody—which he does—except the lyrics. The idea was, I think, to keep Voltaire, but they didn't. But everyone ended up good friends except John Latouche, who died."

There were those who said that if Bernstein did too much, Parker did too little, and for that they were inclined to blame her perpetual partners—Haig and Haig—though Bernstein himself found her "very sweet, very drunk, very forthcoming."

In fact, she had *two* lyrics in the original production but one of them—"Two Hearts So True"—was cut on the road. The song that survived was a quartet:

THE VENICE GAVOTTE
(Quartet: The Old Lady, Candide, Cunegonde, Pangloss)

OLD LADY:	I've got troubles, as I said: Mother's dying, Father's dead. All my uncles are in jail.
CANDIDE:	It's a very moving tale.
OLD LADY:	Though our name, I say again is Quite the proudest name in Venice, Our afflictions are so many, And we haven't got a penny.

CANDIDE: Madam, I am desolate
              At your fam'ly's tragic state.
              Any help that I can give . . .
              Please do tell me where they live.
              I shall look them up tomorrow
              And alleviate their sorrow
              With a check made out to bearer.
              In the meantime, *buona sera*.
CUNEGONDE: We've got troubles, as she said:
              Mother is dying, Father's dead.
              All her uncles are in jail . . .
CANDIDE: (*anxious to leave*)
              It's a very moving tale.
CUNEGONDE: Although our name, I say again is,
              Quite the proudest name in Venice,
              All her uncles are in jail.
              It is a very moving tale, a moving tale, a
                 moving tale.
OLD LADY: Although our name, I say again is,
              Quite the proudest name in Venice,
              All our uncles are in jail,
              It is a very moving tale, a moving tale, a
                 moving tale.
CANDIDE: (*edging off*)
              Ah, what a tale!
              Ah, what a moving tale!

(*They exit together. PANGLOSS emerges through the crowd with a masked PAQUETTE on his arm and flanked by a chorus of ladies.*)

PANGLOSS: Millions of rubies and lire and francs
              Broke the bank, broke the bank.
              Broke the best of all possible banks.
              Pieces of gold to the ladies I throw
              Easy come, easy go.

Shining gold to the ladies I throw.
See them on their knees before me.
If they love me, can you blame them?
Little wonder they adore me.
Watch them woo me as I name them:
Lady Frilly,
Lady Silly,
Pretty Lady Willy-Nilly,
Lady Lightly,
Lady Brightly
Charming Lady Fly-By-Nightly.
My Lady Fortune found me.
What a joy to have around me
Lovely ladies, six or seven;
This is my idea of heaven.
Fortune, keep the wheel a-spinning, spinning,
They adore me while I'm winning.
Lady Frilly,
Lady Silly,
Pretty Lady Willy-Nilly,
Lady Lightly,
Lady Brightly,
Charming Lady Fly-by-Nightly.
Fools love only one or two
Ladies, I love all of you

(*Enter* CUNEGONDE, *the* OLD LADY, CANDIDE, *all still masked. They reprise their earlier songs in counterpoint. Screams of recognition when their masks are knocked off.*)

CUNEGONDE: Ah, Candide!
OLD LADY: Ah!
CANDIDE: Ah! Cunegonde!
PANGLOSS: Ah!
             (*They exit*)

> STELLA: Writing a play should be like robbing a bank.
>   Meticulously planned and worked on in secrecy.
>
> (The Ice Age)

The show that should have made all concerned for their fortunes ran for only seventy-three performances. It was, she remembered, "so over-produced that you couldn't tell what was going on at all," and, indeed, there does seem to be a fatal flaw there somewhere since the two major attempts to revive the piece have fared no better than the original.

From her teens, she had been nursing "vaguely theatrical ambitions" of an unspecified nature, but there is no evidence that Dorothy Parker—Playwright took pen in hand until after she had been fired as Dorothy Parker—Critic.

That came in late 1922, when, oblivious to the reception of *No, Sirree!*, the Algonks decided to put on a full-scale revue called *The Forty-Niners*. Parker and Benchley concocted a sketch called "Nero," which contrived to include a solitaire-playing Cardinal Richelieu, Queen Victoria, the Generals Lee and Grant, and the New York Giants. It was seen just fifteen times—which was the length of the commercial run.

Two years later, she decided to write a full-length play. Once again, the raw material was drawn from her own life—or, rather, on her observation of Robert Benchley's. For the more than a quarter century they knew each other; he was her best friend and soul mate:

FOR R.C.B.

Life comes a-hurrying,
Or life lags slow;
But you've stopped worrying—
Let it go!

Some call it gloomy,
Some call it jake;
They're very little to me—
Let them eat cake!
Some find it fair,
Some think it hooey,
Many people care;
But we don't, do we?

When they both first became involved with the Round Table, Benchley was a militant teetotaler, but it was not long before he fell off the wagon and was leading the social parade. Despite this, he remained married to Gertrude, his wife of many years, and would maintain his home with her and their two sons.

In Mrs. Parker's eyes, this little piece of suburban domesticity was an utter sham, and she enshrined it in her first short story, "Such a Pretty Little Picture." She revisited the subject when she came to start her play *Soft Music* and found the material flowing from her typewriter instead of taking its usual constipated course.

She showed the first act to a producer friend, who advised her that it needed work and suggested he find her a seasoned collaborator. The man he came up with was Elmer Rice, often referred to at the time as "America's Ibsen." He had enjoyed a huge critical success with his expressionistic play about our mechanized society, *The Adding Machine*.

Frankly, Rice needed the money and readily agreed to work with the neophyte playwright. She was "so proud" to be working with him, and they soon developed a working method where she would do the writing and he would help with the all-important construction of the piece.

"I was just trembling all the time, because Elmer Rice had done so many good things, and here was I, a small cluck." How could they possibly fail?

One reason was a little thing called personal chemistry. Rice appears to have pursued his concept of collaboration way beyond the professional. Since he was not handsome or stupid, it was presumably his ruthless pursuit that finally made her agree to go to bed with him a few times—when she found him to be, as she would say later, "without question the worst fuck I ever had."

The play was the story of a mild suburban husband, dominated by a saccharine shrew of a wife and a whining daughter, who discovers the spark of his manhood in the friendship of the ex-showgirl who lives next door. Convention and commitment are finally too strong to allow him to leave, but by the final curtain the worm has most definitely turned.

Since this was her first play, Mrs. Parker chose to follow its out-of-town tryout. She was not impressed with what she saw and declared the play "insipid." When at the dress rehearsal the director Arthur Hopkins began to worry about the unfettered and mobile bosom of the actress playing the showgirl, he asked Dorothy, "Don't you think she ought to wear a brassière in this scene?" "God, no. You've got to have *something* in the show that moves."

She characterized his laissez-faire attitude toward the actors as "the Arthur Hopkins honor system of direction." Nonetheless, she found the experience of watching her work come to life fascinating.

By the time the play opened in New York, its title had been changed to *Close Harmony*, and she was sufficiently encouraged by its reception to organize an opening-night party at The Algonquin. The critics were predictably kind. Who, after all, wished to incur the Parker wrath? The public, however, were less inclined. They withheld their praise and their presence.

The play's commercial chances were not helped by scheduling its first night to coincide with Fred and Adele Astaire's opening in the Gershwins' *Lady, Be Good*.

After a disastrous matinee in the third week, she sent Benchley a cable: "CLOSE HARMONY DID A COOL NINETY DOLLARS AT THE MATINEE. ASK THE BOYS IN THE BACK ROOM WHAT THEY WILL HAVE."

The play closed in New York after twenty-four performances. It then went on a lengthy tour (as *The Lady Next Door*) in which it was just as successful as it had been pre-Broadway. But it was Broadway that mattered to Dorothy. In later years, she found it difficult to discuss what had happened, merely apologizing for the fact that "it was dull. . . . How do you know about your own? . . . You have my apologies."

Nevertheless, she would still maintain that she liked "to do a play more than anything. First night is the most exciting thing in the world. It's wonderful to hear your words spoken."

Mrs. Parker and Mr. Benchley once came close to writing a full-length play together—only a succession of highballs came in the way.

The year 1926 saw Benchley determined to settle down to some serious writing after what he saw as the diversion of his Broadway revue stint. He took a room in the Royalton Hotel, literally across 44th Street from The Algonquin—a geographical mistake in itself—and there he and Mrs. Parker settled down to write their play.

To begin with, they thought they had found an original shorthand way to construct it. Instead of names, their characters would initially have numbers—1, 2, 3, 4, and so on. They soon found that stage directions such as "1 moves upstage, while 2 shrinks against backdrop" had more in common with chess than theater.

Then—their play hardly begun—Benchley received the call to go to Hollywood. Mrs. Parker decided to keep the room and promised Mr. Benchley that she would "hold the fort—so long as I can drink with the Indians." The Indians proved so thirsty that she soon gave up the room.

She tried again in the early years of her marriage to Alan. The theatrical trade press in late 1939 spoke confidently of Guthrie McClintic's forthcoming production of *The Happiest Man*—their adaptation of Miklos Laszlo's original Hungarian play. It would star Ruth Gordon and Walter Huston . . . no, Burgess Meredith . . . no Paul Muni with Otto Preminger producing. In the event—no event.

It was 1947 in Hollywood before she would try again.

Once again—perhaps not surprisingly, all in all—the subject matter was not exactly upbeat. *The Coast of Illyria*—the reference being to the imaginary place where Shakespeare shipwrecks his characters in *Twelfth Night*—dealt with the life of the demented Mary Lamb and included a drugged-up DeQuincey, Coleridge, and, of course, brother Charles. Almost all the characters had at least one fatal flaw or antisocial habit connected to drink or drugs. It was an environment in which the author would, by this time, have felt completely at home. Reading it today, it also becomes clear that the main strand of the piece was drawn from her own destructive relationship with Alan Campbell. "I am Mary Lamb. Do you see that?" she said to the actress playing the part.

This time her collaborator was Rosser (Ross) Evans, who possessed all the other Parker qualifications. Sadly, he lacked any writing ability, but he *could* type—and he had one other thing to recommend him that she had observed on first meeting him; he was almost always drunker than she was. Naturally, they became lovers.

The play was put on in Dallas for a three-week run in April 1949, the critics paying it fulsome compliments and rating it even more favorably than Tennessee Williams's *Summer and Smoke*, which had also premiered there.

Mrs. Parker was again overjoyed. There was talk of Broadway and a production at the Edinburgh Festival. The play was to be retitled *Strange Calamity* or perhaps *The Incomparable Sister*—no, it would be *Mary Is from Home*. And then—nothing.

The relationship with Evans ended unpleasantly a few months later, and she went back to Alan. Later she would conclude, "*Coast* was just plain silly. It was so full of atmosphere that there was nothing else in it. Nothing happened at all, nothing whatever."

Collaboration became something of a social gambit with Dorothy. Joseph Bryan III was a young southern aristocrat she met at a party. He had recently contributed an article to *The New*

MARY: In spite of all our friends in the audience, the hisses drowned out the applause.

CHARLES: Hisses always do. They come more deeply from the heart . . . I joined in the hissing. I was so damnably afraid of being taken for the author.

(The Coast of Illyria)

Yorker and—since he was young and good-looking—"little Mrs. Parker" couldn't have been more impressed. Shooing the other guests away from her immediate vicinity, she sat Bryan down and looked at him soulfully.

"I've just met you, and here I am about to ask you a favor. It's not will you collaborate with me on a play, but how soon can you start?"

They arranged to meet at her apartment the following morning, but when the eager young collaborator arrived, it was clear that not only had she forgotten what they were to meet about—she didn't even remember meeting him.

Her last produced attempt was in every way her most successful, once again a collaboration (with playwright Arnaud d'Usseau): *The Ladies of the Corridor.* D'Usseau was an old friend and political colleague from Hollywood days. When they met again at a New York party in 1952, she asked him the obligatory question one writer asks another: What was he writing?

Jokingly, he replied that he was about to start working on a play with Dorothy Parker. "That's strange," she replied. "Only the other day I was discussing an idea for a play I'm planning to write with Arnaud d'Usseau."

She would claim that they started by working on a murder mystery, but "we dropped it when we found we liked the murderers too much."

In fact, she had been nurturing an idea inspired by her own stay in a residential hotel, the Volney. Changing the name of the hotel to the Marlowe, she and d'Usseau began to work.

It was to be about ladies in retirement. "[They] are not young. But they take excellent care of themselves, and may look forward to twenty good years, which will be spent . . . doing what they are doing in the present, which is nothing at all. . . . They should be better trained" [she added censoriously], "adjusted to live a life without a man." She saw it as a feminist play with the message that women should "stop sitting around and saying 'It's a man's world.'"

In her introduction to the text, she writes, "The theme of *The Ladies of the Corridor* is the wasted lives of these women who live alone in small residential hotels throughout the United States. They have plenty of money and more than plenty of time; their only occupation is to spend one and kill the other. . . . Mostly they are widows (there are over seven million widows in the United States), some less fortunate are divorced, and there's an infrequent nondescript who is only separated . . . [it] is told in a series of scenes, and though the subject is a sad one, the ladies themselves, some on purpose, provide an appreciable amount of humor."

The humor, however, is frequently painful and personal, and one does not need to stretch far to see the fifty-nine-year-old Dorothy Parker in more than one of the characters.

There is the separated Mildred Tynan.

"Mildred is perhaps thirty-five; she is small and delicately made and she must have been an extraordinarily pretty girl; now there's a strain and an apprehension about her, but she keeps a curiously touching charm that should have somebody to protect it."

Mildred's problem is alcohol. Drink "makes you a different person. You're not yourself for a little while, and that's velvet. . . . A couple of drinks and I've got some nerve. Otherwise I'm frightened all the time." With the self-pity, though, goes a self-deprecating black humor. "I'm giving up solitaire. I can't win even when I cheat. . . . Maybe I could give music lessons to back-ward children? . . . I finally got so I could play "The Minute Waltz" in a minute and a half."

Then there is Connie Mercer, whose husband deserted her.

"He found somebody who was young for the first time. So then there was a succession of transients [for me]. . . . The one-night stands don't do any good. I found that out. There's got to be fondness and there's got to be hope."

Mildred would agree.

"I couldn't believe things could ever be rotten. . . . Well, I kept hoping, hoping. I'm the damnedest hoper you ever saw in your life . . . I can hope about anything."

The Ladies of the Corridor opened on Broadway in October 1953. Critic George Jean Nathan then hailed it as the best play of the year.

For Dorothy, there was one major disappointment. After the opening, the producer, Harold Clurman, insisted on changing the suicide ending she had written to give the play a final note of hope. "It wasn't right, you see . . . I had written a very bitter play, but true. . . . It was the only thing I have ever done in which I had great pride."

Clurman's decision may well have confirmed the play's fate, for it closed forty-five performances later. But maybe the fact that it *was* so palpably true was what also made it too painful to watch. Nathan called it "completely honest." To paraphrase George S. Kaufman on satire, "Honesty is what closes in six weeks."

The near success—as the authors saw it—encouraged them to have one more try. *The Ice Age* was a depressing story of a weak, handsome man dominated by his mother. He goes to work in an art gallery, where he is seduced by the sadistic gallery owner, whom he eventually kills.

In it—for those familiar with her life—were her feelings toward Alan's mother, Hortense, and her concerns over his (as she saw it) ambiguous sexuality. It was both too personal and not sufficiently original for the Broadway of 1955. Producer Robert Whitehead took up an option, more out of kindness to Dorothy than through any real conviction in the play. In due course, he let the option quietly drop, and that was that.

The verdict on Dorothy Parker—Playwright must surely be that she was the victim of her own tragicomic vision, a vision that prevented her from writing either pure comedies or undiluted tragedies. She left her audiences in two minds—a state that would have been unmercifully lampooned by Dorothy Parker—Critic.

More successful than any of the plays Dorothy Parker wrote were the plays written *about* her. Actress Ruth Gordon (*Over 21*, 1930) and Mrs. Parker's publisher, George Oppenheimer (*Here Today*, 1932), both incorporated a Parkeresque character in their plays.

Asked whether she would ever contemplate writing an autobiographical play, Parker replied, "No chance. If I ever wrote a play about myself, George Oppenheimer and Ruth Gordon would sue me for plagiarism."

"Rose-Colored Bifocals": Parker and Politics

I cannot tell you on what day what did what to me.

—Dorothy Parker

My heart and soul are with the cause of socialism.

—Dorothy Parker

They were progressive days [the 1930s]. We thought we were going to make the world better—I forget why we thought it, but we did.

—Dorothy Parker

Stop looking at the world through rose-coloured bi-focals.

—Dorothy Parker's advice to a young reactionary

These are not the days for little, selfish, timid things. . . .
Oh, the years I have wasted being a party girl and
smartcracker, when I could have been helping all the
unfortunate people in the world.

—Dorothy Parker

ALTHOUGH SHE couldn't put a specific date to the
moment when she felt the first stirrings of social conscience, 1927 would seem to be as good as any, for that
was when she took her first positive action.

Women had won the vote in 1920, but so far Dorothy had
not taken the trouble to vote herself. Politicians of both parties
left her cold, and it was not until after Franklin Roosevelt was
elected that she is known to have expressed a positive opinion
on one.

"He was God; you didn't exactly feel you were slumming
with him."

But perhaps his consort, Eleanor, made the FDR ticket especially attractive to a woman like Dorothy Parker.

"What a woman. . . . It's hard to believe, but when you met
her, she was the most beautiful woman you ever saw."

The incident that triggered Parker's political activism was the
long, drawn-out affair of Nicola Sacco and Bartolomeo Vanzetti—
a fish peddler and a shoemaker by trade but self-styled "anar-
chists" by persuasion. They had been arrested seven years earlier
and found guilty of two murders in Massachusetts. Now all the
legal maneuverings were exhausted, the two men were on death
row, and their execution date was fixed. To a lot of people—many
of them famous—this was an appalling miscarriage of justice,
and they were determined to stop it, even at the last minute.

Mrs. Parker made the train journey to Boston and insisted
on marching in the parade of dissent. She was warned by the
police and finally arrested but not before she had felt the ugli-
ness of the crowd turned in her direction with shouts of "New
York nut!" "Red scum!" and "Hang her!"

She found the experience of her first arrest a distinct anti-climax. No one even took her fingerprints. "But they left me a few of theirs, the big stiffs!" she said, showing the bruises on her arms where the policemen had frog-marched her to the jail. For the reporters, she managed a typical Dorothy Parker crack after she had been released on bail: "I thought prisoners who were set free got five dollars and a suit of clothes."

The execution was delayed but finally carried out. But there was one other consequence of the Boston trip. The federal authorities began to compile a dossier on Dorothy Parker.

Back in New York at the Round Table, things were never quite the same for her. Having had her own conscience disturbed, she found it hard to accept the way her colleagues seemed so unconcerned with the way the world was going.

"Those people at the Round Table didn't know a bloody thing. They thought we were fools to go up and demonstrate for Sacco and Vanzetti . . . they didn't know and they just didn't think about anything but the theatre."

All she knew was that injustice in any form made her "wild," and as the country lurched into depression, she saw plenty of it.

It was a time when many a liberal mind saw a great deal to admire in the Russian experience with communism, and the Parker toe was dipped into the political water—though there is no firm evidence that she ever joined the Communist Party.

Certainly, she attended a number of rallies in those succeeding years; but as a literate person, she found the speeches "much too long and much too muddy and with many—too many—sweeping allusions to the woiking class and the bawss class."

In Hollywood in the 1930s, she found a focus for her "wild" feelings. To begin with, there were many like-minded liberals. With her old Algonk colleague and now a successful screenwriter Donald Ogden Stewart, Fredric March, and Oscar Hammerstein II, she helped found the Hollywood Anti-Nazi League in 1936—something that would come back to haunt her twenty years and a whole world later. But at the time, "It is my pride that I can say that Donald Stewart and I and five others were the organizers. . . . From these seven it has grown in two years to a membership of four thousand . . . and it has done fine and brave work."

Despite all the disappointments and frustrations she was to encounter over the next decade, this aspect of her work released something within her and gave her genuine satisfaction. "[It] makes me proud to be a member of the human race, and particularly proud to belong to the women's division of it."

The other issue was even closer to home. She may have hated writing for the screen herself, but she was prepared to expend significantly more energy than went into her scripts to defend the rights of others to do the same. She helped set up the first trade union for screenwriters—the American Screenwriters Guild—and served on the board.

"I saw some of the stinkiest practices you'd ever want to see. People—honest, hard workers—were thrown out of their jobs, without warning, without justice. People were hired on what is called 'spec'—which means that they wrote without pay, with the understanding that if their work was accepted they would be paid. And then their work would be used, but they would be fired—still without pay. . . . Some claimed that every writer received for his trash $2,500 a week. . . . The average wage of a screenwriter was *forty* dollars a week . . . perfectly corking, except that there was a catch to it. The average term of employment was two weeks in a year."

She was realistic about the attitude of the studios and even the "Academy" (of Motion Picture Arts and Sciences). Expecting them to protect the rights of writers was "like trying to get laid in your mother's house. Somebody was always in the parlour, watching."

She was equally realistic about what was involved in selling such a revolutionary idea to her fellow writers.

"Now, look, baby, 'union' is spelled with *five* letters. It is *not* a four letter word. . . . The bravest, proudest word in all the dictionaries is 'organize.'" But even so, "if a screenwriter had his name across the Capital Theatre in red, white and blue letters fifty feet tall, he'd still be anonymous."

There were other lessons they had better learn right away, and one of them was to relate to the new reality of the world they were living in: "Writers could not find themselves until they find their fellow man. Moon, death, and heartbreak are personal matters, but the songs of my time are dead."

Hollywood also brought her face to face with racial discrimination—a subject that preoccupied her to the end of her life. In 1930s Hollywood, a black actor would almost always play a kindly comic servant with rolling eyes and shuffling gait.

When Mrs. Parker was asked to appear in a charity sketch with one of the better-known ones in which the stereotype would once again be employed, she steadfastly refused. "Black people have suffered too much ever to be funny to me."

She would bitterly lampoon the white attitude in her short story "An Arrangement in Black and White" as a well-meaning but insensitive southern lady explains her husband's "liberal" attitude: "But I must say for Burton, he's heaps broader-minded than lots of these Southerners. He's really awfully fond of colored people. Well, he says himself, he wouldn't have white servants."

Looking back in the early 1960s, she would summarize the range of her humanitarian views: "Acceptance is what hurts you in all forms. . . . You get soft and don't stand up on your hind legs. When the day comes that you can accept injustice, anywhere, you've got to kill yourself."

In November 1937, she made a pilgrimage in pursuit of her convictions. The Spanish Civil War was raging. Back home, it was chic to debate it and to take the Loyalist side. Many of her friends set off for Spain, but, as she was to witness in person, few got farther than the border. Dorothy, as an accredited correspondent for the left-wing publication *New Masses*, went considerably further and wrote, "I want to say first that I came to Spain without my axe to grind. . . . I am not a member of any political party. The only group I have ever been affiliated with is that not especially brave little band that hid its nakedness of heart and mind under the out-of-date garment of a sense of humor. I heard someone say, and so I said it too, that ridicule is the most effective weapon. I don't suppose I ever believed it, but it was easy and comforting and so I said it. Well, now I know. I know that there are things that never have been funny, and never will be. And I know that ridicule may be a shield, but it is not a weapon. . . .

"I don't see how you can help being unhappy now. The humorist has never been happy, anyhow. Today he's whistling past worse graveyards to worse tunes. . . . There is nothing funny in the world any more. . . . If you had seen what I saw in Spain, you'd be serious, too. And you'd be trying to help these poor people."

And what she saw was that "the streets are crowded and the shops are open, and the people go about their daily living. It isn't tense and it isn't hysterical. What they have here is not morale, which is something created and bolstered and directed. It is the sure, steady spirit of those who know what the fight is about and who know that they must win. . . .

"But I, as an onlooker, am bewildered. . . . [In Madrid] in spite of all the evacuation, there were still nearly a million people here. Some of them—you may be like that yourself—won't leave their homes and their possessions, all the things they have gathered together through the years. They are not at all dramatic about it. It is simply that anything else than the life they have made for themselves is inconceivable to them. Yesterday I saw a woman who lives in the poorest quarter of Madrid. It had been bombed twice by the Fascists; her house is one of the few left standing. She has seven children. It has often been suggested to her that she and the children leave Madrid for a safer place. She dismisses such ideas easily and firmly. Every six weeks, she says, her husband has forty-eight hours leave from the front. Naturally he wants to come home and see the children. She, and each one of the seven, are calm and strong and smiling. It is a typical Madrid family."

But elsewhere, her emotions were put to the test. She visited children in refugee camps. "They don't cry. Only you see their eyes. While you're there and after you're back, you see their eyes. . . .

"While I was in Valencia the Fascists raided it four times. If you are going to be in an air raid at all, it is better for you if it happens at night. Then it is unreal, it is almost beautiful, it is like a ballet with the scurrying figures and the great white shafts of the search-lights. But when a raid comes in the daytime, then you see the faces of the people, and it isn't unreal any longer. You see the terrible resignation on the faces of the old women, and you see little children wild with terror. . . .

"Last Sunday morning, a pretty, bright Sunday morning . . . there was a great pile of rubble, and on the top of it a broken doll and a dead kitten. It was a good job to get those. They were ruthless enemies to Fascism."

One story came out of her experiences in Spain. Almost documentary in style, "Soldiers of the Republic" tells of two women in a café who meet a group of Loyalist soldiers returning to the front. They chat and give the soldiers their cigarettes, and then the soldiers leave. When the women try to pay, they find the soldiers have already bought their drinks. It was an incident that actually happened to Dorothy Parker, and she never forgot it.

"It was darling of me to have shared my cigarettes with the men on their way back to the trenches. Little Lady Bountiful. The prize sow."

Of the Spanish people, she said, "They ask only as much as you have because they are people like you . . . they want to live in a democracy. And they will fight for it, and they will win."

That was what she hoped but didn't really expect to happen.

"You knew darn well it was going to happen, even when you were there." She took the Fascist victory badly. "I die hard."

Of those who died, she said, "Few of their names are told, and their numbers are not measured. They wear no clean and carven stones in death. But for them there is an eternal light that will burn with a flame far higher than any beside a tomb."

And at a public meeting on her return, she was still emotional: "I cannot talk about it in those days. All I know is that there I saw the finest people I ever saw, that there I knew the only possible thing for mankind is solidarity . . . their defense against the invasion of the Fascist has failed. But do you think that people like that can fail for long, do you think that they, banded together in their simple demand for decency, can long go down? They threw off that monarchy, after those centuries; can men of ten years' tyranny defeat them now? I beg your pardon. I get excited.

"It is no longer the time for personal matters—thank God! Now the poet speaks not just for himself but for all of us—and so his voice is heard and so his song goes on."

By 1939, she could see that the enemy, as she defined it, was within the domestic gates. She told the Left Wing Congress of American Writers, "For heaven's sake, children, Fascism isn't coming—it's *here*! It's dreadful. Stop it!"

But it was only a matter of months before her own world fell in pieces. The nonaggression pact signed by Germany and Russia left her disillusioned with left-wing causes, and she resigned from all her affiliations on the spot. Her cause was still right, but her solution was clearly wrong, and surely everyone else would feel the same.

She was highly critical of those who refused to see the light as she did. For people like Walter Duranty, the Moscow correspondent for the *New York Times*, she had nothing but scorn: "When the train of history went around a sharp curve, he fell out of the dining car."

By this time, however, the damage was done. The FBI already had an extensive file on Dorothy Parker, and when she applied for a permit to be a war correspondent, it was refused. "Possible subversive" and "premature anti-Fascist" were two of the descriptions that she would never be allowed to see but that influenced that decision and others that would follow after the war.

The activities of the House Un-American Activities Committee (HUAC)—under the rabid direction of Senator Joseph McCarthy and Judge Parnell Thomas—constituted one of the most shabby episodes in immediate postwar American history. Its self-appointed mission was to root out communist influences in American life, and its principals decided that show business in general and Hollywood in particular would give them an immediate high public profile. And if it took a little exaggeration to make the point, then so be it.

Many talented people on both sides of the camera had their careers effectively ruined by maintaining their constitutional right to privacy. Some even went to prison. Had she been a man, Dorothy Parker would probably have been one of them, for her attitude toward the committee was contemptuous throughout.

When she received a subpoena in 1952, she referred to the committee members as "rats gnawing at empty holes"; and when they asked her about her activities in the 1930s, she replied, "I haven't the faintest idea about the politics of Hollywood in the 1930s, and you make me laugh when you speak of them. . . .

"Are you now or have you ever been a member of the Communist Party? I was and am many things, to myself and to my friends. But I am not a traitor and I will not be involved in this obscene inquisition." She did not, she said, "even understand what a Communist organization was."

But perhaps the most typical Parker response was to the FBI: "Look, I can't even get my dog to stay down. Do I look to you like someone who could overthrow the government?"

Time and again, she took the Fifth Amendment. Finally, the committee gave up and sent her home. "I was black listed. I couldn't get another job." All around her, she sensed fear like "the smell of the Black Plague."

"The infallible Sam Goldwyn said, 'How am I to do decent pictures when the good writers are gone to jail? Don't misunderstand . . . I think they ought to be hung.' "

She could no longer work in Hollywood, but who the hell wanted to, anyway? The only trouble was that the "seriousness" of her purpose had rubbed off on her prose since the late 1930s. She had begun to find that, politics apart, editors were rejecting her work unless it was humorous. It became her excuse for writing less and less.

"My work is dismissed, and on the strength of what seems to me a curious adjective—'unpleasant.' The last editor, who may as well be nameless because he has all the other qualities of a bastard, told me that if I changed my piece to make it in favor of Franco, he would publish it. 'God damn it,' he said, 'why can't you be funny again?' "

There was *almost* a different ending. In 1961—when a little
sanity had been restored both to the nation and to the
Parker household—she returned to live with Alan Campbell in
Hollywood, having remarried him a decade earlier. For Alan, this
was like the second professional coming. Assignments for which
he would not normally be considered might open up, if they
were a writing team again.

Their old friend Charles Brackett was currently the head of
Twentieth Century Fox, and he wanted to develop a mildly successful play, *The Good Soup*, as a vehicle for the studio's major
star, Marilyn Monroe. He decided to ignore the blacklist.

To their disappointment—though hardly to Mrs. Parker's
surprise—it was Hollywood business as usual. "Everybody's
a writer and has ideas. . . . We wrote a nice, little, innocent
bawdy French farce . . . [the play was a translation from La Bonne
Soupe] . . . and they took our script and hoked it up with dope
pushers, two murders and, straight out of Fanny Hurst, the har-
lot with a heart of goo."

In the end, it scarcely mattered. Monroe was coming apart by
the day. She had two films left to make on her Fox contract. In the
summer of 1962, she was fired from the first, and a month later
she was dead. So were the Parker/Campbells as screenwriters.

If I had a shiny gun
I could have a world of fun
Speeding bullets through the brains
Of the folk who give me pains;

But I have no lethal weapon—
Thus does Fate our pleasure step on!
So they still are quick and well
Who should be, by rights, in hell

("Frustration")

"Did Ernest Really Like Me?"

Did Ernest really like me?

> —Dorothy Parker to her friend
> Beatrice Stewart Ames just before her death

Half across the world from me
Lie the lands I'll never see

> —"Hearthside"

Paris was where the twentieth century was.

> —Gertrude Stein

Even though it happened in France, it was all some-
how an American experience.

> —Gerald Murphy

Songs Just a Little Off Key

By

Dorothy Parker

Portrait of the Artist

OH, lead me to a quiet cell
  Where never footfall rankles,
And bar the window passing
  well,
And gyve my wrists and ankles.

Oh, wrap my eyes with linen fair,
  With hempen cord go bind me,
And, of your mercy, leave me there,
  Nor tell them where to find me.

Oh, lock the portal as you go,
  And see its bolts be double. . . .
Come back in half an hour or so,
  And I will be in trouble.

Experience

SOME men break your heart in two,
  Some men fawn and flatter,
Some men never look at you;
  And that cleans up the matter.

Inscription for the Ceiling
of a Bedroom

DAILY dawns another day;
  I must up, to make my way.
Though I dress and drink and eat,
Move my fingers and my feet,
Learn a little, here and there,
Weep and laugh and sweat and swear,
Hear a song, or watch a stage,
Leave some words upon a page,
Claim a foe, or hail a friend—
Bed awaits me at the end.
Though I go in pride and strength,
I'll come back to bed at length.
Though I walk in blinded woe,
Back to bed I'm bound to go.
High my heart, or bowed my head,
All my days but lead to bed.
Up, and out, and on; and then
Ever back to bed again,
Summer, Winter, Spring, and Fall—
I'm a fool to rise at all!

Unfortunate Coincidence

BY the time you swear you're his,
  Shivering and sighing,
And he vows his passion is
  Infinite, undying—
Lady, make a note of this:
  One of you is lying.

Philosophy

IF I should labor through daylight and
  dark,
  Consecrate, valorous, serious, true,
Then on the world I may blazon my
  mark;
  And what if I don't, and what if I
  do?

Autobiography

OH, both my shoes are shiny new,
  And pristine is my hat;
My dress is 1922. . . .
  My life is all like that.

OROTHY PARKER did not leave the United States
until the summer of 1926, when she was thirty-two. It
was strange for someone of her surface sophistication
and intellectual curiosity—especially when so many of her
friends had been flocking there since the war. Europe—and
France in particular—was considered exotic. The franc was cheap,
the liquor flowed freely, and, besides, all one's friends were there.

Even so, it took eight years to winkle her out of the security
of New York City, and she made sure she could take a good
part of it with her—in her case, Mr. Benchley. She also took her
current lover, Seward Collins ("I ran off to the Riviera with a
Trotskyite").

The year 1926 was "the golden summer," "the summer of a
thousand parties," Scott Fitzgerald called it. He and his wife,
Zelda, were just two of the gliterati she would run into in Paris
and on the Riviera, where the social life revolved around the
"golden couple"—American expatriates Gerald and Sara Murphy—
and their Villa America on Cap d'Antibes, where the parties were
lavish and seemingly endless.

Americans of that time and type preferred to hunt in packs,
and the unstated object of the overseas exercise was to colonize
"abroad" and turn it into "home." The Riviera, for instance, they
found to be "a darned good little dump."

Mrs. Parker would chronicle this aspect of it in her 1929
story "The Cradle of Civilization" as "two young New Yorkers
sat on the cool terrace that rose sharp from the Mediterranean,
and looked into deep gin fizzes":

"Their costumes seemed to have been assembled in compliment to the general region of their Summer visit, lest any one
district feel slighted; they wore berets, striped fishing-shirts,
wide-legged cotton trousers, and rope-soled *espadrilles*. Thus, a
Frenchman, summering at an American resort, might have
attired himself in a felt sombrero, planter's overalls, and rubber
hip-boots. . . .

"[A local] kept screaming all this stuff about why did these
Americans come over here, anyway. And there was Bill . . . yelling

right back at him, 'Yes, and if we hadn't come over, this would be Germany now.' I never laughed so much in my life. . . .

"[The French are] so damn dumb, they make me sick. Why, they don't even speak English at the post-office."

Dorothy Parker wrote little about her several trips to Europe in the 1920s and 1930s—perhaps because she did, indeed, feel that she was part of a touring company taking a New York show on the road and rehearsing the same predictable lines.

On that first trip, she had promised herself that she would use the new and untainted environment to settle down to some serious writing, but the temptations proved too great. Instead, she drank even more. When critic Edmund Wilson met her on her return, he found her "fat and bloated, puffy-eyed." ("Why dontcha ever come to see me, yuh damn fool?")

She found herself a minor character in a play with some larger-than-life characters. There were the Scott Fitzgeralds. She'd met Scott first. "He told me he was going to marry the

"I have friends who have traveled much in France. They tell me the people are French wherever you go. What an over-whelming effect that must have!"

(Charles Lamb in *The Coast of Illyria*).

We long to lay down for her all we have;
We love her, we love her, la belle, la brave!
We'd see given back to her all her due—
The grandeur, the glory that once she knew.
We'd have her triumphantly hung with flowers,
Acknowledged supremest of all the Powers,
Her dominance written in white and black . . .
But, boy, we'd be sore if the franc came back!

("Song of American Residents in France")

most beautiful girl in Alabama *and* Georgia." Mrs. Parker first met the two of them in a restaurant where the seats were lined up against the wall. "It looked like a touring production of The Last Supper." As a couple, they seemed to have "just stepped out of the sun, their youth was striking . . . they were the golden lad and the golden girl, if ever I saw them." Though when she knew them better, they seemed to be "both of them too ostentatious for words . . . their behavior was calculated to shock."

Nonetheless, she had to admit, "*Everyone* wanted to meet them. *This Side of Paradise* may not seem like much now (1964) but in 1929 it was considered an experimental novel; it cut new ground. . . .

"Zelda: I never found her very beautiful. She was very blonde with a candy box face and a little bow mouth, very much on a small scale and there was something petulant about her. If she didn't like something, she sulked; I didn't find that an attractive trait." Though what Parker initially saw as petulance might very well have been the early signs of the dementia that eroded so much of her later life. Being thrown so much into her company, the rest of her set had to learn to cope with her unpredictable behavior, which could often drift into the bizarre.

"She was living in the day of the shock technique. That wears off quickly, don't you think? Sitting at a dinner where nothing in particular was being said, she would turn to a neighbor— 'Ah do think Al Jolson's a greater man than Jesus Christ, don't you?' She wanted to be thought of as 'fast'—A speed." Most of Zelda's later life was spent in one sanitarium or another with her husband struggling to pay bills that far exceeded the royalties from his novels and stories.

Scott himself fulfilled many of the Parker criteria for the acceptable male—and, inevitably, they had a token fling in the mid-1930s. But as many people found when they got past the Fitzgerald facade, there was a lot less there than met the eye.

"Scott was attractive and sweet and he wanted to be nice . . . but the damnedest thing about Scott, he didn't know what was funny. He could be funny in his books but not about life."

It was Fitzgerald, however, who definitively captured that fleeting moment for all time in his 1934 novel *Tender Is the Night*, in which all the principal characters are based on his friends from the south of France.

Over the years, Mrs. Parker and Fitzgerald drifted apart. Ironically, however, their lives and careers drifted in parallel since both of them turned up in Hollywood at the end of the 1930s, frittering away their talent and drinking heavily.

Fitzgerald died suddenly of a heart attack in December 1940, his talent and reputation reduced to a shadow. At the funeral parlor, Dorothy Parker came to pay her last respects. Leaning over the open coffin, she shocked the other mourners. "The poor son-of-a-bitch!" Only a few of them recognized that she was quoting the words of a mourner at the funeral of Jay Gatsby, Fitzgerald's most famous character.

By this time, the gilt had long since worn off the golden girl and lad. "Ah, hell," Parker wrote in an unpublished letter, "if I were a God, I'd *be* a God."

"It wasn't the parties that made it such a gay time. There was such an affection between everybody. You loved your friends and wanted to see them every day, and usually you did see them every day. It was like a great fair, and everybody was so young" (Sara Murphy).

Dorothy Parker certainly loved the Murphys. None of her friends escaped the edge of her tongue at some point—except the Murphys.

Gerald was heir to the profitable Mark Cross leather goods empire, and Sara, his senior by several years, also came from money. An unlikely couple when they married in 1916, they became the still center of their many interlocking circles of friends, particularly in Europe, where they were one of the first couples to put down roots.

With Gerald's artistic eye—he was to develop into a highly regarded painter—and Sara's sense of esoteric good taste, the

Murphys set the unofficial standards for a new American–European style of living.

Over the years, Mrs. Parker grew close to them as a family—to the point where, when their elder son, Patrick, was suffering from tuberculosis in 1929, she accompanied the "Swiss Family Murphy," as she called them, to the live-in hotel/clinic in Montana-Vermala.

She positively hated Switzerland itself. It was "the home of horseshit," where everything was built "on the side of a God damn Alp." The Palace Hotel did little to make her feel better. To suit the needs of its patrons/patients, the temperature had to be kept "fresh." "What you wear for dinner is a tweed suit, a coat over it, a woolen muffler tied tight around your neck, a knitted cap, and galoshes. When you go outdoors, you take off either the coat or the muffler."

Nor was there much on offer by way of entertainment. She found herself fascinated, she wrote to Mr. Benchley, by a towel pinned over her washstand.

"It's a good thing to look at. You can go all round the edges very slowly, and then you can do a lot of counting the squares made by the ironed-out creases."

Because of her genuine affection for the Murphys, this atypical Good Samaritan stayed longer than anyone could have expected and was a positive help in her own disorganized way. But the pull of a polluted New York finally overcame the pure Swiss air, and, besides, it was time to earn some money. She was so overdrawn that her account looked "positively photographic." She declared that all she wanted to do was to "return to a vine-covered country cottage and spend the rest of my life raising checks."

"When the day comes that you have to tie a string around your finger to remind yourself of what it was you were forgetting, it is time for you to go back home."

She would remain close to the Murphys, though, for the rest of their lives. Years later, she was on her way to dinner with them in the company of Lillian Hellman, who had met them in Paris in the late 1930s. It is the only recorded barb Mrs. Parker is known to have fired at either Murphy, and it was harmlessly blunt.

She bet Hellman that she could guess "who Gerald will have discovered this time—what writer, I mean." She made three guesses—Madame de Staël, Gerald Manley Hopkins, and "Philippe de Swartzberger . . . an Alsatian who moved to Tibet. Born 1837, died 1929, or so it's thought. A mystic, most of whose work has been lost, but two volumes remain in Lausanne under lock and key, and Gerald invented him this afternoon." After dinner, Gerald produced a slim volume and insisted on reading from it. It was by Hopkins.

There was one rather less cheerful encounter some years earlier. One evening when Murphy picked her up for dinner, he found her with a black eye and other evidences of her having recently been in the wars. As they drove off in the taxi, she explained that her current aristocratic stockbroker lover had beaten her up the previous night.

"How can you bear that man, Dottie? He's a very dirty cad!" Gerald properly complained.

A still drunk Mrs. Parker peered at him and said with great dignity, "I can't let you talk of him that way, Gerald," before opening the taxi door and falling out into the Park Avenue traffic. The man in question was the "whipping boy" who killed himself in the Martha's Vineyard airport some years later.

Apart from the Murphys, the person from those years and that context who influenced her the most was undoubtedly "Old Dr. Hemingstein"—Ernest Hemingway. She met him on that first 1926 visit and was in ambiguous personal and professional thrall to him ever after.

In 1929, she wrote a profile of him for *The New Yorker* in which she called him "far and away the first American artist . . . it is the devil's own task to find anything more complicated or necessary to say about him."

Nonetheless, over the years, she would continue to find things to say—things that defined her own ambitions and fears every bit as much as his.

"Hemingway has an unerring sense of selection. He discards detail with a magnificent lavishness, he keeps his words to their short path. He is, as any reader knows, a dangerous influence. The simple thing he does looks so easy to do. But look at the boys who try it. . . . He is clean . . . exciting."

To Robert Sherwood, she would confide, "We all need heroes, don't we?"

In the profile, she quoted one of Hemingway's own lines, "Scratch a writer and find a social climber," and compared him to other writers she could think of whose ambitions "beckoned toward the North Shore of Long Island." "Hemingway avoids New York, for he has the most valuable asset an artist can possess— the fear of what he knows is bad for him."

In fact, apart from necessary visits to his publishers, Hemingway avoided the United States altogether as much as possible. He would certainly not have been seen dead within a mile of the Round Table. New York writers he considered to be "all angle-worms in a bottle."

"Old Dr. Hemingstein" may have been a hero to Mrs. Parker, but the feeling was not reciprocated. At a Paris party some time after one of her suicide attempts—a party at which she was not present—he offered a toast to the absent lady: "Here's to Dorothy Parker. Her life will never become her so much as her almost leaving it." He appeared unable to understand why the other guests found his remark in poor taste.

Occasionally, Dorothy would force herself to face the truth about her excessively macho friend. Fitzgerald had wanted to be nice, but not Hemingway. "Ernest never wanted to be nice; he just wanted to be worshipped. He was a bore then and he remained so." By the time the Great White Hunter took his gun and blew his brains out in 1961, many people had come to the same conclusion.

Although she sometimes saw truth through her glass darkly, this was not a palatable one. One of the last things she said before her death was to her lifelong friend Beatrice Ames—the divorced wife of Algonk writer Donald Ogden Stewart—who had witnessed the whole saga.

"I want you to tell me the truth. Did Ernest really like me?" she asked and was assured that he had.

The truth of the matter was that Hemingway had realized early in the game that his oversized ego would never allow him to like someone so able to provide him with the commodity he hated most: competition.

When Dorothy and her traveling companions were embarking at Cherbourg on the SS *Rotterdam* to return to New York at the end of that summer of 1926, Hemingway was one of the party seeing them off. Half jokingly, he shouted up to her. He had no typewriter—what was he to do?

Without hesitation, she threw her own brand-new portable down to him. Then, turning to her friends, she said, "Good God, I have just thrown away my only means of livelihood!"

At this remove, the symbolic incident is open to at least two distinct interpretations. She was either throwing a professional lifeline to a man she admired or telling a talented but obstreperous individual to shut up and write. Or possibly both.

Over the years, Dorothy Parker met most of the good, the bad, and the ugly the world considered famous. Some she began by admiring. Somerset Maugham was one of them.

At a dinner party, he asked her to compose one of her verses for him. She wrote,

> Higgledy piggledy, my white hen;
> She lays eggs for gentlemen.

"Ah, yes," said Maugham, he had always liked those lines. She then picked up her pen and added,

> You cannot persuade her with gun or lariat
> To come across for the proletariat.

She so intrigued Maugham that he invited her as a weekend guest. Much to her dismay after her initial excitement at
the prospect, she found herself odd woman out in a gay
enclave. When reporting on the visit, she declared, "That old
lady is a crashing bore," adding for good measure, "Whenever
I meet one of those Britishers, I feel as if I have a papoose on
my back."

Parker legend has it that one of her favorite enemies was some-
time-actress and full-time society beauty Clare Boothe Luce.
(" 'Clare-Boothe-Luce' sounds like the motto of a girls' school.")

When fellow socialite Ilka Chase tried to persuade Dorothy
that her friend Clare was always kind to her inferiors, Parker
asked, "And where does she find them?"

Their most famous exchange was probably apocryphal, but
no matter. The two ladies supposedly arrived together at the
swing doors of the Algonquin. Standing aside to give Mrs. Parker
preference, Clare said, "Age before beauty," to which our heroine
replied, "Pearls before swine." Clare Boothe Brokaw (as she was
at the time of the "encounter") rather reluctantly denied the
story in later years.

Her explanation that "the story probably was worked up as
a suitable piece of dialogue for the two of us by some columnist"
rings all too true, for the practice was prevalent. In any case,
Woollcott had used the exchange earlier in a short story, and
other versions of the encounter substitute Gypsy Rose Lee or an
unnamed "chorus girl" for Luce. Still, as the saying goes, when
the facts differ from the legend, print the legend.

Parker and Clare-Boothe-Brokaw-Luce don't appear to have
been either particular enemies or friends, but someone who
started out as a prickly antagonist and then turned into
an unlikely friend was Lillian Hellman. ("The trouble with
Lillian . . . is she thinks she's Dashiell Hammett—when she only
looks like him.")

In the event, Hellman turned out to be the executor of the
Parker estate, and the two women spent a great deal of time

together in Dorothy's last years, laughing at the foibles of their assorted friends and acquaintances.

Mrs. Parker was never quite comfortable, however, until she had achieved at least one put-down on even her nearest and dearest, and she achieved this one day when she was staying with Hellman. They took a walk to the lake on the Hellman property so that Lillian could inspect her snapping-turtle traps—a practice of which Mrs. Parker thoroughly disapproved. When they reached the spot, her hostess picked up a trap that had a young turtle in it. The tiny creature's penis was erect with fear.

"It must be pleasant to have sex appeal for turtles," said Mrs. Parker sweetly. "Shall I leave you alone together?"

CHAPTER

15

Coda: The Lady of the Corridor

This is my city, this is my town, why did I ever leave it?
—Dorothy Parker on returning to New York in 1963

But I shall stay the way I am,
Because I do not give a damn

—"Observation"

Promise me I'll never grow old.

—Dorothy Parker

If I had any decency, I'd be dead. Most of my friends
are.

—Dorothy Parker on her seventieth birthday

CONNIE: *Only don't let yourself get lonely. Loneliness*
makes ladies our age do the goddamnedest things. . . .
These women are dead and death is contagious.
LINSCOTT: *Life certainly treats you fine.*
CONNIE: *No, Tom. Life and I go Dutch.*

—The Ladies of the Corridor

IN 1963, Dorothy Parker returned to "her" town for the last
time. It was, she declared, "a hell of a place. . . . A silver cord
ties me right to my city."

Alan had died in their Hollywood home and, just before he
did, had said something quite prophetic: "It's the end of the
rainbow for both of us, I fear." He'd said it wryly rather than por-
tentously, and, in any case, how could Dorothy argue, she who
had been keenly anticipating the end from the very beginning?
In turn, she had visualized him as "Betty Boop going down for
the last time."

She settled herself back in the residential Volney Hotel,
where she had stayed before in the 1950s—the inspiration for the
Marlowe in her play *The Ladies of the Corridor*. She had kept her
room there long after she had actually left New York to live in
Los Angeles. She saw it as a sign of her independence. ("I'm a
hobo and I mean to be forever.") But this time it was different.
This time she wasn't just passing through. This time it was for
real and for good.

It was, she told friends, "the kind of hotel where business-
men install their mothers and then run. . . . Do you know what
they do when you die in this hotel? They used to take them
down on the big elevator in the back, but it's not running, and
they take them down in that front elevator, and you know how
small it is. They have to stand you up."

In those last few years, her reputation finally and fittingly
caught up with her, and the honors came thick and fast.

In 1958, the National Institute of Arts and Letters gave her
their most prestigious award and later inducted her into the

institute itself. In recent years, she had become preoccupied with what she called "making it" as a writer, and her acceptance speech reflected it. It was terse, to say the least: "Never thought I'd make it." And she was gone.

Then, in 1963, she was appointed Distinguished Visiting Professor of English at California State College at Los Angeles, an experience she perversely enjoyed and in which she turned her "lectures" into a series of conversations.

Her room at the Volney was monastic in her usual "Hogarthian" style—just she and her dogs. Friends noticed that personal possessions were few. On the shelf were few books and only one of her own—her collected poems. Pride of place on a shelf of its own was a set of thirteen porcelain figurines of Napoleon and his generals that she and Alan had bought in a Santa Monica antique store. Why she valued them so particularly was never entirely clear.

She had run out of things to live for by now. "I'm seventy and feel ninety. If I had any decency, I'd be dead," she would tell people, "because anybody I ever cared about is dead." She said it matter-of-factly, and it never came out as self-pity, something she loathed in others. She remembered the dignity her friend Oscar Levant had displayed in sickness. "He never went around with a begging-bowl extended for the greasy coins of pity." And nor, she vowed, would she, though in the end she had to, for Good Samaritans were getting harder to find.

In her play of a decade earlier, she had recorded some of the experiences that she now witnessed daily being enacted by the players on her personal stage. There were the Lonely Ladies, left unequipped for the future they now faced:

> LULU: I guess there's something lacking in a lot of women. . . .
> We were told you grew up, you got married and there you
> were. And so we did, and so there we were. But our hus-
> bands, they were busy. We weren't part of their lives; and

as we got older, we weren't part of anybody's lives; and yet we never learned how to be alone. . . .

You see, I've learned from looking around me that there is something worse than loneliness and that's the fear of it. . . .

MILDRED: Vegetables: . . . sitting there in their bins, waiting for the garbage collector to come and get them. I think in many cases they're contented women; they wouldn't change places with anyone, and if you possibly told any of them they were miserably unhappy, they'd think you were insane. But some of them don't know they're dead—that curious death in life with which they are content. . . . It's too pompous, I know . . . but I don't think tragedy is too big a word because the waste is unnecessary. . . .

PAUL: Promise me you'll never be seen carrying a lending library book; the book with the cellophane dust jacket. It's the badge of the unwanted woman. . . .

MRS. GORDON: A lady starts staying in her room, after while she gets so she never goes out of it. . . .

PAUL: People don't change, they just get more so.

There would be one last party. Her hosts were Gloria Vanderbilt ("Gloria the Vth") and her husband. Years earlier, Mrs. Parker had written a poem that contained these lines:

Where's the man could ease a heart
Like a satin gown?

Satin glows in candle-light—
Satin's for the proud!
They will say who watch at night,
"What a fine shroud!"

For the occasion, Ms. Vanderbilt provided her with a silk dress (size 3) of yellow brocade with gold trim, encrusted with tiny pearls. It was fully six inches too long, but Dorothy refused to have it shortened. "No, I want it long. Then I have to lift it. I want to have that haughty look." In the evening she wore it, and three months later she was buried in it.

Having been at war with herself and everyone around her all her life, she finally capitulated to a heart attack on June 7, 1967. She was almost seventy-five years old. Her mother had died on a rainy day, and the memory had stayed with her:

Oh, let it be a night of lyric rain
And singing breezes, when my bell is tolled.
I have so loved the rain, that I would hold
Last in my ears its friendly, dim refrain.

June 7 was a gloriously sunny day in the 80s. Now, wouldn't you just believe it!

CHAPTER

16

Envoi: *"As Dorothy Parker Once Said ..."*

As Dorothy Parker once said ...
> —Cole Porter, "Just One of Those Things"

She had a quiet voice, and she said her words with every courtesy to each of them, as if she respected language.
> —"Dusk Before Fireworks"

EVAN: Please call me Evan.
LESTER: All this and Evan, too.
LOUISE: You're slipping, Lester. That was originally said by Dorothy Parker.
LESTER: Everything was originally said by Dorothy Parker.
> —Noël Coward, *Long Island Sound*

I shall come back without fanfaronade
Of wailing wind and graveyard panoply;
But, trembling, slip from cool Eternity—
A mild and most bewildered little shade.

—"I Shall Come Back"

Four be the things I am wiser to know:
Idleness, sorrow, a friend and a foe.

Four be the things I'd been better without:
Love, curiosity, freckles and doubt.

Three be the things I shall never attain:
Envy, Content, and sufficient champagne.

Three be the things I shall have till I die:
Laughter and hope and a sock in the eye.

—"Inventory"

THE CLUES to the question, "Who was Dorothy Parker?" are all there in her own verse and fiction, almost begging to be found. For much of her life, she was a public figure, and she was as ambivalent about her fame as she was about just about everything else.

"How would you like to walk into a party and have a dozen women look up and say with their eyes, 'So *you're* Dorothy Parker. I dare you to say something nasty.'" (Which begs the obvious question, Why *go* to the party?)

"I certainly must be cutting a wide swathe through this party. I'm making my personality felt. Creeping into every heart, that's what I'm doing. Oh, have you met Dorothy Parker? What's she like? Oh, she's terrible. God, she's poisonous. Sits in a corner and sulks all evening—never opens her yap. Dumbest woman you ever saw in your life. You know, they say she doesn't write a word of her stuff. They say she pays this poor little guy, that lives in some tenement on the lower Eastside, ten dollars a week to write it and she just signs her name to it. He has to do it, the poor devil, to help support a crippled mother and five brothers and sisters; he makes buttonholes in the daytime. Oh, she's terrible."

Wyatt Cooper titled his *Esquire* appreciation "Whatever You Think Dorothy Parker Was Like, She Wasn't." It was an appropriate premise because she certainly polarized people.

To those who suffered from her pen, her tongue, or her turned back, she was "a sour little girl who was always going around slashing her wrists." To those with the patience and insight to see past the self-defensive mannerisms, she was one of the defining literary talents of the first half of the twentieth century and—although she would have hated the thought—probably the most influential writer about what it was to be a woman in that changing time.

She played her own part in ensuring that confusion was worse confounded. The messages she sent out about her own life were mixed. Few people heard exactly the same story—and never twice. It was her way of keeping her personal life personal. One would be told that all her best friends called her "Dorothy"; another would hear "Dottie." At the time, she probably believed either or neither.

Perhaps the explanation was that she didn't see life as a continuum but as an unconnected series of piercing insights:

"It's life, I suppose. Poor little things, we dress, and we plan, and we hope—and for what? What is life, anyway? A death sentence. The longest distance between two points. The bunch of hay that's tied to the nose of a tired mule."

"I suppose that's the one dependable law of life—everything is always worse than you thought it was going to be."

"Melancholy is the act of remembering."

"They sicken of the calm, who knew the storm."

She claimed to live by simple axioms.

There were two things one should never trust—"a round garter and a Wall Street man"—and there were two things she could never comprehend—"how a zipper worked and the exact function of Bernard Baruch." (The latter frustration was shared by most people at the time.)

She was well aware of how people saw her. But, then, they didn't understand.

"Don't sit alone and dramatize yourself. Dramatize yourself! If it be drama to feel a steady—no, a *ceaseless* rain beating upon my heart, then I do dramatize myself."

Dramatize—and defend . . . against anybody and everybody. Just in case. She embraced Swift's credo that "I have ever hated all nations, professions and communities and all my love is towards individuals. . . . But principally I hate and detest that animal called man; although I heartily love John, Peter, Thomas, and so forth."

"I do it in defence, I suppose. . . . If I didn't say nasty things, I'd cry. I'm afraid to cry; it would take me so long to stop."

Barbed words were a defensive perimeter for Dorothy Parker, but she was perfectly well aware that they were not in and of themselves of any permanent significance. "Frankness, if you will forgive dogma, is no synonym for honesty." And, of course, you couldn't "teach an old dogma new tricks."

Didn't she enjoy *anything*? she was often asked. "Flowers, French fried potatoes and a good cry," she answered on one occasion—but the next time she probably said something quite different.

But through the cracks (of both kinds) and against a mountain of contrary evidence, one is inclined to believe that she meant it when she said, "I am the greatest little hoper that ever lived," even if she never quite knew what she hoped for and certainly expected to be disappointed with it if she ever got it.

"To say that Miss Parker writes well is as fatuous as saying that Cellini was clever with his hands," was Ogden Nash's verdict. Alexander Woollcott was predictably more orotund. Her writing was "so potent a distillation of nectar and wormwood, of ambrosia and deadly nightshade, as might suggest to the rest of us that we write far too much." André Maurois called her "the American Colette"—a considerable compliment in Gallic context—while her contemporary, critic Edmund Wilson, concluded, "Her wit is the wit of her particular time and place, but it is as often clearly economic at the same time as it is flatly brutal . . . it has its roots in contemporary reality."

True enough, but the roots continued to grow long after the "contemporary reality" died back.

> Travel, trouble, music, art,
> A kiss, a frock, a rhyme—
> I never said they feed my heart,
> But still they pass the time.
>
> ("Faute de Mieux")

What Dorothy Parker saw and committed painfully to paper was a more timeless reality—or she would by now be no more than a dusty footnote to a brief episode in the social and literary culture of a single city.

We are fortunate that she lived at a moment when the Great Minority of Women was finding its feet and searching around for its feminist place in the brave new postwar world. All that choice—but what to choose? And apart from the battle of the sexes, what was happening to the *balance* of the sexes? All of this she saw while she was scrabbling around to find her own place to stand.

And perhaps her greatest accomplishment was that, while society grudgingly gave women a vote, Dorothy Parker gave them a voice. She showed American women that it was permissible to be self-assured, outspoken, bold, and witty—to be proud to have a mind and to speak it in whatever words came to it.

And it would be nice to think that at the end she realized that her deepest wish had been granted. Nobody any longer thought that she wrote "like a woman."

> But I, despite expert advice,
> Keep doing things I think are nice
> And though to good I never come—
> Inseparable my nose and thumb.

Index

About the Author

BARRY DAY is the author or editor of numerous books, plays, and musicals. As longtime consultant to the Noël Coward Estate, he has written extensively on Coward, including editing *The Complete Lyrics, Theatrical Companion to Coward, Coward in His Own Words, Complete Sketches,* and *The Unknown Noël.* He is currently engaged in editing *The Noël Coward Letters.*

He is a director of the International Shakespeare Globe Centre and was one of the team that helped Sam Wanamaker rebuild that historic playhouse on London's Bankside. His book, *This Wooden 'O': Shakespeare's Globe Reborn,* is the official account of the project.

The series of "literary autobiographies" under the title *In His Own Words* also includes Oscar Wilde, P. G. Wodehouse, and Sherlock Holmes. He has also published *The Complete Lyrics of P. G. Wodehouse.*

Born in England and an Oxford M.A., Barry Day, his wife Lynne, and dog Sonny spend their time between New York, Westport, Connecticut, and Palm Beach, Florida.

First day cover of the Dorothy Parker stamp, August 22, 1992.